I DREAM LIKE YOU
STORIES WE WALK PAST

Edited by Saker Mistri

RUPA

Published by
Rupa Publications India Pvt. Ltd 2018
7/16, Ansari Road, Daryaganj
New Delhi 110002

Sales centres:
Allahabad Bengaluru Chennai
Hyderabad Jaipur Kathmandu
Kolkata Mumbai

ISBN: 978-81-291-5133-9

First impression 2018

10 9 8 7 6 5 4 3 2 1

The moral right of the author has been asserted.

Printed in India by Replika Press Pvt. Ltd.

I DREAM LIKE YOU

*For Shaheen who had the vision
and all the teachers and volunteers
who help her realize it*

CONTENTS

FOREWORD

It is hard and messy to sum up twenty-five years of Akanksha. I've grown up with her, and growing up *is* hard and messy. Akanksha's children have been my children; their journey was my journey. They have challenged me, stunned me, fuelled me and showered love upon me.

Akanksha started as a very ordinary story—a little dream, really. I was 18, in my first year of college, and wondered why the students didn't seem to notice the many things around us, which seemed so wrong to me. Over curry-rice and chai in the St Xavier's College canteen I learnt that my friends did want to solve some of the problems they saw, but didn't know how to go about doing it. To create awareness about social problems, I went from class to class, armed with a hand-painted poster that said—'You Can Make a Difference'.

The idea was simple: bring together college students who had time, kids who needed an education and classrooms that were empty after regular schools ended. The result was: the first Akanksha Centre. Volunteers ran from college to the community, collecting kids, teaching them songs and games on the bus and together entering a classroom in the Holy Name School, Mumbai—excited and nervous—everyone ready to learn.

Over the years, the fifteen kids who we tried to keep in class and stop from running to the bathroom where they would jump into the basins with running water—a novelty for them—grew to over 7,000 students. Today, full-fledged Akanksha schools help put every child on the path to college and a life of their choice. We've encountered some unpredictable challenges in our path— an NGO which spread rumours that we fed vegetarian kids non-vegetarian biryani, superstitious parents who refused to take their kids to the doctor, a school principal who complained that our kids' clothes smelled of fish and their bangles scratched her school furniture. But there was a flip side—slivers of joy—the child who finally got medical attention, the school that gave us a cupboard to store our educational material, volunteers who defied parents who were convinced that teaching slum kids was a 'waste of their time'. With each little step forward, our dreams for our children became bigger. One centre became sixty centres and the centre model morphed into the school model.

Enter any Akanksha school today and you will see it was worth every obstacle we had to face. Chess players line the long corridors, in the cheerful libraries children engage in discussions on problems in the community while other kids engage in the School Review Process to bring changes in their schools. At Akanksha, we teach children, not classes; we believe in interdependence not independence. We are driven by a singular purpose—the unleashing of a child's greatest potential, irrespective of his or her background.

There are few jobs where your heart *breaks* as often, making it difficult to know what to do. It was not easy to explain to Bharati and Gitanjali that they could still be friends and that the world was still good—even though one of their mothers got a life sentence for burning the other. It was not easy to sit in Ashish's little room, under the fan from which he hung himself while his mother proudly showed me his drawings and offered me tea.

But there are few jobs where your heart *fills* as often with hope. Anjali's students did a two-hour commute to learn at her centre. Prashant's mother valued education so much that she encouraged him to sit for his final exam even though his father had passed away that same morning. There isn't an office in the world where no matter how you performed the previous day, you enter each morning to watermelon-wide smiles, sparkling eyes and a welcome of 'Hi, Didi'.

Hope and truth have kept me on this path all these years. As you read these twenty-five incredible stories, hold the thought in that hand-painted college poster I made twenty-five years ago—'*You* can make a difference'. In our next twenty-five years, Akanksha will leap forward—for and with our children—to bring our audacious vision from the hope that it is, to the truth that it must be. We must work together, tirelessly—for an excellent education is the right of every child in our nation. And if my journey is anything to learn from, I promise in that quest you will get back infinitely more than you give.

Shaheen Mistri
Founder, The Akanksha Foundation

INTRODUCTION

In my search for twenty-five young men and women who have overcome enormous challenges and transformed their lives, I discovered many more than twenty-five stories. In a ripple effect, each narrative opened up another one, and another, and another: stories of their teachers, mothers, fathers, mentors, employers and friends, a network of stories that grows around each one of us as we create our own.

The experiences of the writers in the book take place within two parallel worlds, divided by invisible and at once distinct lines: the bitter realities of the slum communities they live in, and the rich opportunities of Mumbai and Pune, the cities to which they belong. Each story is different, yet through them runs a common thread: all have been students at Akanksha, a non-governmental organization that educates children from low-income communities. And from their collective experiences emerges another powerful narrative—the story of Akanksha.

What was it that enabled these twenty-five alumni and hundreds more like them, to go beyond the limiting conditions into which they were born? How did they transform the shackles of their childhood—crippling poverty, physical abuse and humiliation in school—into incentives for change?

'Sometimes I wonder how it all happened,' says Sumeet, an alumnus who went on to found the Pragati Holistic Development

Trust. 'Was it the respect of the volunteers and mentors who never bothered that I was from a scheduled caste? I know that at Akanksha I never felt like a "*sharabi ka bachcha*" (son of a drunkard).'

A sense of self-confidence is reinforced by the responses we evoke around us. It was only after they were accepted and valued for who they were, that the writers discovered self-worth, and took pride in their achievements. Rewards, small and big— stars for creative drawing, an award for attendance, a college scholarship—gave them courage to redraw their own images.

It is easy and often convenient to stereotype low-income communities as the 'unfortunate underprivileged'. Jyoti, now a film-maker, strips off her label, 'I am not underprivileged. I am privileged compared to my friends who are already married, to my mother who was abandoned as a child and had to eat from dustbins to kill her hunger, to those who never had the opportunity to go to college like I did.'

Role models were absolutely essential to such transformation. While distant icons in magazines and Bollywood films fired their imagination, the real inspiration came from those within everyday reach. Didis and bhaiyas—their teachers— set high goals both for their students and themselves; they found time to build relationships, motivate academic achievement and counsel on appropriate behaviour. The ultimate role model was the mother. As a wife she was often helpless and abused, but as a mother she rose to protect and support her children with an inborn faith that was formidable.

The bedrock of education at Akanksha is value-based knowledge. The primary focus is—as it should be—on individual students; the curriculum comes second. Children from low-income families need as much art, music and poetry as those in private schools. Amit, a student of science, defines what education now means to him: 'To be truly educated, I must explore the social, creative and intellectual ingredients within myself.' With meaningful learning, the writers grew out of the narrow and fear-laden mindsets bred in many municipal schools—and into the limitless expanse of thinking, imagining and questioning.

Values cannot be superimposed. Personal experiences demonstrate that values were assimilated and reinforced through stories in class, experiences on field trips and the actions of their mentors. Both positive and negative situations helped children figure out that what was acceptable to them—what gave them a sense of well-being—was valued by them. Love, respect and friendship made them feel good—and they worked to assimilate core values.

The fire to succeed, to cross that poverty line, motivated the writers to put a huge premium on hard work. They stretched their days to fit in a job, long hours of study, difficult commutes and sports training. Mahesh L., a chartered accountant, worked out a formula for himself: 5 = 50, *five years of hard work = fifty years of enjoyment*! The supreme goal for all the writers was to be financially independent and support the family. Seema, a school principal, recalls, 'The most memorable moment was when I got a part-time job after Class 12, and took on the family responsibility, so my mother had to no longer go out to work.'

Sadly, there were many children who fell short of their aspirations. Families relocated to distant suburbs or towns and parents were not always supportive. Often, school and Akanksha timings clashed, making it impossible for students to attend, while some were forced to stop their studies to earn a living.

I found it difficult at first to understand the strong desire of nearly all the young adults to give back to a society that had given them so little. But somewhere along the way, feeling empowered by the opportunities they had, alumni—often jointly—initiated their own 'giving back' projects: community classes for children, programmes in hospitals, renovations in broken-down schools. Everyone has something to give.

The need for reform in our government education system cries out of every story. Poorly qualified and uncaring teachers have traumatized generations of Indian students. Government officials, heads of institutions, scholars and researchers have frequently questioned the poor state of India's schools and come to their own conclusions. The input of students—the receivers of the education—is rarely asked for or given consideration. How can children be motivated? Which teaching methods bring the best learning? What are the attributes of a good teacher? In this book the students give us some honest and revealing answers.

India's larger social issues—gender discrimination, forced early marriages and corruption—together with a disadvantaged family environment—parental physical abuse, alcoholic fathers and demolition of homes—can play havoc with young lives. The environment at Akanksha was the positive balance the children needed, and today the writers are able to reflect on these hardships with compassion and an understanding that is way beyond their years.

There are no new themes in these stories, only those that time makes stronger: love, loneliness, success, fear and freedom; themes that cut across gender, class, geography and cultures. Each of us will find some connection at different points in the narratives, for the reader's journey is not too unlike the writer's. The need to hope, dream and achieve brings us both together—no matter where we were born.

Saker Mistri

SALMAN SAYYED | AKANKSHA | 2007 TO 2013
BA final year, Kishinchand Chellaram College, Mumbai
Tour Guide and Office Administration, Magic Tours India
Date of Birth: 3 December 1992

BORN ON THE PAVEMENT

I was born on the pavement in Mumbai, next to a bus stop at the junction of four major crossroads. On the opposite side of the road stood the Haji Ali Juice Centre, as busy twenty-five years ago as it is today. Hindu–Muslim riots had broken out all over the city, and Ammi, my mother, could not get to a hospital. It was around 5 o'clock in the morning on 3 December 1992, and the situation must have been very frightening for her. Years later, the unusual place of my birth became a huge problem, for no one was ready to issue me a birth certificate and there was no written evidence that I was born. It was only at the age of 24, after I won a court case, that I officially began to exist!

The Haji Ali junction was our home. Day and night, cars honked, crowds walked past and red double-decker buses threw out black smoke. We lived in a tent: a plastic sheet that was tied at one end to the top of a municipal garden railing, and the other end fastened to large stones on the street. The sloping plastic prevented the rainwater from collecting over us and the stones stopped the tent from flying away in the monsoon winds. At night, the street lamps shone through the plastic, lighting up the inside of the tent.

We slept on thin blankets, and in the morning, everything we owned—spare clothes, cooking pot and spoons—were tied into bundles and hidden in the bushes or behind garbage cans, so that they were not stolen or taken away by the Brihanmumbai Municipal Corporation (BMC) workers who cleaned the streets. Sometimes we moved the tent to Kutta Wadi, on the large rocks opposite the posh National Sports Club of India (NSCI). And sometimes we camped at the end of the road that led to the Regional Transport Office, outside the golf course of the fancy Willingdon Sports Club.

My Abba's (father's) parents came from Gujarat, and like so many migrant families, set up a home wherever they could. Unfortunately, unlike many of them, we did not 'move up' in line, remaining where we started two generations ago—at Haji Ali junction. Ammi, Shaheda Sayyed, and Abba, Iqbal Gulab Sayyed, had a love marriage at Haji Ali itself. Ammi had only attended primary school and left her studies because she had to do all the household chores for my two elder aunts. Abba has never been to school, but can write in Hindi and English, and speaks a few local languages that he learnt while working in different jobs.

The crossroads became my school. Abba taught me my first ABCs, and wanting to read the advertisements on the large billboards, I was eager to learn more. But Ammi was not keeping well, Abba could never stick to any one job and my sister had left us to work as a housemaid—I had to start earning to help feed the family. My childhood friend, Nasir, suggested I sell books at the Haji Ali intersection, where traffic jams are common and cars halt for a longer time. It seemed the perfect place to launch my 'signal career'. I was 11 years old, and my first sale was a Sidney Sheldon novel that I sold for ₹130, making a ₹50 profit. The first day I earned a total of ₹170!

The *Time Out* magazine owners paid us a daily wage of ₹85 plus a commission of ₹5 for each magazine we sold. I was super happy—I was on my way to financial independence. Now I could look after my mother and see to it that she no longer went hungry at night. I enjoyed chatting with motorists who drove by and because I liked talking to foreigners, my friends called me 'Angrez' (Englishman). Customers often helped me to read the book titles, and my friends and I would hold competitions on who could read the maximum number of words on the advertisement hoardings.

As my vocabulary increased, word spread that the Angrez could read! One morning, walking towards the public toilet, I saw a group of my friends talking to two women in a park across the road. 'Angrez,' Yusuf called out loudly, 'come over here.'

As I walked towards them, Yusuf pointed to me, 'Angrez is good at reading.'

The women were from The Akanksha Foundation and asked me to read for them. I was just a 'roadside learner', but they were surprised at the way I had taught myself to read. 'Come to the Akanksha Centre,' they said, 'we will help you to read even better.'

One of the women, called Caroline, asked me, 'Salman, who do you think is happier—the rich or the poor?' My reply came quick, 'The poor are happier. They have no money to lose and no cause for worry. The rich must rush off to work before the boss arrives. Look at me, I sleep and wake up whenever I like and don't think about tomorrow. I am happy with my life.' My answer, based on my idea of happiness, must have interested her, for she asked me again to attend her classes.

I was 14 years old and my life on the street was not bad at all. There were always friends hanging around to play goti (marbles), spin tops or hit a cricket ball. I slept under the stars, ate what food was given to me, or what my earnings could buy. I did not need a school or advice. Akanksha classes began at 9 a.m.—too early in the morning for me, I never woke up before 11 a.m.! Many non-governmental organizations (NGOs) had tried to get me off the streets and into school. I did not need to be saved!

But curious to find out more about this Akanksha, I went to the Worli Centre. Caroline Didi was really happy to see me. The class started with a prayer. Looking back, I laugh when I think how I misunderstood the words of a song the students were singing. The line was, 'Thank you God for the world so sweet,' and I thought they were singing, 'Thank you God for the girls so sweet!' My English was okay for selling books but I could not understand what was going on in the class, I felt uncomfortable, and spoke only to Caroline Didi. Maybe, Akanksha was not for me...

After a few weeks or perhaps it was months, I stopped going to the Centre, but Caroline Didi did not stop coming to Haji Ali. No matter how many excuses I made for not being in class, she did not give up, and, like Google, she searched everywhere until she found me! We would sit on the footpath, on the wall along the sea or in the public garden where I had first met her, and talk about different things.

My biggest excuse for not going to the Centre was that it started too early. One morning, Didi herself came to wake me up, and feeling ashamed, I followed her to the Centre. For the next few days she came every morning to make sure that I got to class on time! Akanksha even sent me a letter saying I could arrive later than the other students! Afraid I would be forced to attend regularly, I did not reply and for a whole year was absent from the Centre. My parents, happy that I was earning well, did not even try to make me study.

Life on the street had a timetable of its own. Every morning, we stood in long lines outside the Haji Ali Mosque to get dal gosht (meat and lentils), and my favourite bhuna chawal (meat and gravy with rice), which was distributed to the poor. On Friday mornings, we ran to the Hindu Santoshi Mata Temple at Mahalaxmi and sat in a circle, waiting for the sweet, milky kheer, puris (fried puffed bread) and channa (chickpeas) that the priests distributed to the poor. One day followed another, with no fixed time for anything, except going to the madrasa, where we recited aloud verses from the Quran and were punished each time we mispronounced a holy word.

We were four siblings, and one winter my mother had taken my older sister and brother, Shaheen and Shahezad, and the baby Seema, to visit an aunt in Ajmer. In the cold climate of Ajmer, Seema died. Ammi returned to Mumbai leaving Shahezad and Shaheen with my aunt. After she left, my aunt started beating them and they ran away to the safety of the dargah of the saint Khwaja Gareeb Nawaz. There, they met an unknown 'aunty', who brought them to Mumbai. Arriving in Mumbai, tired and hungry, the aunty sent Shaheen to buy some food. When she returned to the spot where she had left them, both aunty and my brother had disappeared! We never saw Shahezad again. In just two months, two members of our family were gone.

Shaheen and I were enrolled in the BMC school in Mahalaxmi but we both dropped out to begin working—she in Class 3 and I after Class 2. On festival days, Shaheen painted henna patterns on women's hands and feet; I helped at the roadside juice stalls. Ammi was a part-time housemaid. She made extra money collecting plastic and other materials that washed up on the beach when the tide went out, and sold these to the bangar-wallahs (junk collectors). Often, she would wake up at 4 a.m. to gather the more valuable scrap materials, before the other ragpickers began their rounds. However, the money was never enough, and we regularly went begging outside the Haji Ali dargah.

Abba photographed tourists who visited the Haji Ali Mosque, which is built far into the sea, or did other temporary jobs. His work depended on his many moods. He was an alcoholic—a king in his own world—and came home drunk practically every day and beat my sister, mother and me. I still don't know the reason for this daily punishment. Once he threw a sharp pointed comb at my sister and it actually struck her in the forehead!

Maybe there were some long-term benefits in those beatings, because the fear of Abba's bad temper kept Shaheen and me away from the drugs and violence on the streets.

My mother's support was the only positive influence in my childhood. She prayed hard for things to get better for my sister and me, and tried to protect us from our father's abuse. Her life was tough, in frustration, she sometimes hit us with any object that she got her hands on.

Everyone stopped at Haji Ali's 'Bada signal'—actors, cricketers, writers and film directors. Milind Soman, the model; Ashwin Sanghi, the author; Rahul Kadri, the architect; and Zayed Khan, the actor, were all friendly. Actor Jackie Shroff even spoke our street language! Sachin Tendulkar, Ravi Shastri, M.S. Dhoni and my cinema heroes—Hrithik Roshan and Salman Khan—drove past. Many of them bought my books and I started giving credit to regular customers. After Nasir and Mustak, I was the third best signal bookseller. My income grew steadily and I spent a big part of it on late-night movies. On Fridays, the book owners paid for our movie tickets: an incentive for us to sell more. I lived each day as it came and never thought about the future. Only late at night, in the darkness of the air-conditioned movie hall where the light from the big screen lit up our faces, my friends and I escaped into the world of Bollywood.

One afternoon, one of my customers stopped to talk to me. He explained the many benefits of education and strongly encouraged me to start school. Caroline Didi had told me the same thing many times but that day a light bulb flashed in my head: only a good education could get me a good job and money to buy the scooter of my dreams.

Caroline Didi welcomed my comeback to Akanksha. 'It's your Centre,' she said, 'come whenever you like.' A typical Akanksha student wore the Akanksha T-shirt; I dressed in my usual clothes, kept my earrings on, but agreed to cut my long hair, of which I was very proud. My attendance was irregular, but when I went, I was punctual. Caroline Didi even offered to pay for my transport so that I was in time for class but I refused her offer. Instead, with my savings, I bought a bicycle and cycled to the Centre.

Now that I wanted to study, everything was different. From discovering that 'wo-man' was a lady and not another type of man, I soon progressed to reading comic books and solving arithmetic and algebra problems. But geometry continues to give me a headache! I shared my new knowledge with my street gang and enjoyed the superior status it gave me!

My motivation to study became stronger and I prepared for the National Institute of Open Schooling Class 10 examination. To qualify, I needed a Class 8 certificate, but I had only passed

Class 2! Even though I was fully prepared without the required certificate, I could not sit for the exam. Again, Caroline Didi worked tirelessly and got me the documents I needed.

My days were full. I sold books early in the mornings, studied at the Akanksha Centre or Caroline Didi's house from 10 a.m. to 6 p.m. and again sold books until late at night.

During the Class 10 exams, seeing that I was nervous, Caroline Didi came daily to pick and drop me to the examination centre. While waiting for the final result, I set up a stall selling costume jewellery in the subway at Haji Ali, and worked at actor Rahul Bose's NGO, The Foundation. Unfortunately, the results were very disappointing. I had failed in mathematics and therefore failed in the whole examination. But I was not going to give up. I started studying all over again, and thanks to Vandita Didi's tutoring, I cleared the finals in my second attempt and got admission in the Commerce stream at Navneet College. It was June 2011 and I was 19 years old.

Talking to motorists had improved my general knowledge and speaking skills. In college, I was comfortable discussing different subjects with students and professors—never too shy to compliment the female teachers. If one of them looked good, I was the first one to tell her, 'You look beautiful, Miss!' At night, I continued to sell books, not ashamed to wave out to friends who drove past. Rakesh Bhaiya and Rohan Bhaiya—from Akanksha—helped me in Accounts and other subjects. I enjoyed every minute of college life, and was nominated the Best Student of the Year for two years running, with scores of 91 per cent and 81 per cent, respectively. In the second year of Junior College I was made the Head Boy.

I have always followed my heart, and after two years of

studying Commerce, I transferred to the Arts and Humanities Department at Kishinchand Chellaram (KC) College where I never dreamt that I would get admission. Thanks to a loan from Ridhima Didi (she does not want it returned, but I shall definitely repay her) and a scholarship from Akanksha, I am now in the final year of my Bachelor of Arts (BA) degree, majoring in sociology. My aim is to get a Master's degree in sociology from a college in the United States (US).

Over the years, some amazing people have entered my life, but Caroline Didi tops the list. Didi has curly hair and is always simply dressed in jeans and a kurta. She has been a second mother to me—the first person who showed interest in my life. She made me believe that I had the ability to do something of value—praising me when I deserved it, and pulling me up when I went wrong. I call her President Caroline because she has been the president of my life. I have never told her all this, but reading my story, she will know what she means to me.

When I was younger, I dreamt of joining the Indian Army and much later did apply, but failed the physical test. With time, dreams change, today I no longer want a military career—there are other dreams to fulfil.

The Social Leadership Programme (SLP) at Akanksha motivated me to do something about the inequality in our society. I interned at Harsh Mandar's Aman Biradari, an NGO in Delhi that educates street children, and was impressed with 'Night Walk', their medical aid van that patrols the streets to help the homeless. The SLP introduced me to Rohit Bhaiya, the first true adult male friend I ever had. He taught me to develop a critical mind, to respect different perspectives and not to accept things at face value.

The rapes, killings, and the gender, caste and social discrimination in India upset me a lot. Mahatma Gandhi's policy of non-violence worked well in the past, but today, punishment for wrongdoers must be severe and speedy. It is the children who will make a peaceful world. My association with NGOs like Hamara Foundation, Child Line and Magic Bus, has inspired me to start an NGO for kids at Haji Ali. They will be encouraged to go to school and lead a better life. Seeing me, some of these children are already inspired to study further. I am also a mentor to my sister's three children.

After college and over weekends, I work as a tour guide and help with office administration at Mumbai Magic, an Indian tour company. My NGO, too, will be a travel company, where kids will be trained to be tour guides while continuing with their studies. They will have opportunities to meet new people and explore new places.

Abba's pattern of living has not changed but I understand him better. He has every right to live his life the way he wants. I too have lived by my rules. Ammi continues to work as a housemaid, but now I support my parents, and they have moved off the streets and into a rented room in Kalyan. Soon, I plan to buy a permanent and safe house for my mother. Perhaps the hard realities that I had to face can best be understood as a 'required event' in my life—that is the way I like to think about it.

In 2016, I was selected to speak at Akanksha's 25th Anniversary Gala dinner in New York (NY). I was super excited, but because I had no birth certificate or a permanent address, I could not apply for a passport. I filed and won a court case, was issued a birth certificate, and after going to the police station exactly twenty times for verification, I finally got my passport made.

But that was only the hurdle to the first step. The event was on 10 May 2016, but the earliest available US visa interview was on 9 May. There was no way I could get the visa the same day as the interview! My dearest friend, Robin Chaurasya, somehow arranged for a 5 May appointment date and my application was accepted. But before the visa was approved, there was a Police Clearance Certificate (PCC) to be submitted, and the passport to be picked up. It was my twenty-first visit to the police station! I said to myself, 'Oh, come on! Not again!'

The PCC was a long drawn-out process. Firoze Bhaiya, my second saviour, worked some magic and organized for me to pick up the passport from the office in Nasik. I caught the midnight train, arrived in Nasik at 4 a.m., appeared at the passport office at 9.30 a.m., got the PCC, rushed back to Mumbai and went straight to the American Consulate. But problems are my best friends. I had all the documents, but when I got to the Consulate, their computer system wasn't working! I asked, 'God, why are you playing with me?' The next two days were the weekend and the Consulate was shut. On Monday morning, 9 May, I was back at the Consulate, the first person in the queue, but my passport was not there! I begged them to check and recheck until at last it was found! A few hours later, I was on my first plane trip to New York—the city of my dreams.

I stepped out at Kennedy Airport, into the coolest weather. After Mumbai's scorching 35 degrees, the 12 degrees was heaven! I was in the US, the feeling was totally beyond what I had imagined.

At the Gala dinner, I went up to the stage to speak in front of 250 people—heads of corporations, Akanksha's NY Board, wealthy private donors and leaders in the field of education. I looked at the guests in front of me—everyone was new, everyone had a very different background from mine. I was nervous, exhausted, but so happy that I had made it. I told them my story like it happened and got a standing ovation. I stepped down from the stage, and all my emotions came tumbling down in tears—tears straight from my heart. I thought of my supporters and didis, especially Caroline Didi. I silently thanked Shaheen for the lovely Akanksha tree she had planted twenty-five years ago. I am one of the thousands of children—the fruits of that tree. It was a moment that I will remember for the rest of my life.

The next day, I walked around the city: visiting the City of New York Museum that I knew about from Google; and the 9/11 Museum where the memory of the victims is kept alive, their shoes, caps and other objects on display. There was always something going on in Times Square—the lights flashing day and night.

Unlike Mumbai, NY is a planned city, but like Mumbai, everyone is always rushing to reach their destination on time! People followed rules in NY and men did not just stand and pee anywhere they liked! New Yorkers cared about their city, in India we misuse our facilities—one of the reasons they are always breaking down! We can't even look after the dustbins on our streets! Unfortunately, our mindset is such.

But there was too much wastage of food and water in the US. At every meal, food, more than I could eat, was put on my plate—I could never finish it. Perhaps, many Americans have not known what it is to be hungry, and so are not aware that every grain of rice is precious.

I travelled to New Jersey by train where my hosts, Gauri Didi and her husband, Paul, lived. Wow! What a train! I met inspiring and knowledgeable people—Gauri Didi, Fali Sir, Xerxes Sir, Ashish Sir and Paul Sir. I caught up with my tutor, Rohan Bhaiya, and some of the tourists I had met in Mumbai.

On my bucket list was a ferry ride on the river, to watch the sunset over the Manhattan skyline. I got on to the boat, passed Ellis Island and the Statue of Liberty, and saw the sun going down over the city. It looked beautiful from all sides. NY is the city of opportunities, and one day soon, I will go back there to get a Master's degree. I spent eight wonderful days in NY and then boarded the plane to come back to India, where I know I belong.

∽

'Perhaps the hard realities that I had to face can best be understood as a "required event" in my life—that is the way I like to think about it.'

YASHODHARA SHERKAR | AKANKSHA | 2008 TO 2013
BA final year, Baburaoji Gholap College, Pune
Cyclist, Maharashtra Team
Date of Birth: 3 January 1998

CYCLING INTO THE FUTURE

My first bike was an ordinary one—black in colour, with brakes that were not too good. But that ordinary bike changed my life. My father, Bhau, bought it for my brother and me to share, and we competed to see who could learn to ride it first. It took me only a few minutes to get my balance right, and then I proudly rode around, as if I had won a world championship! Being physically fit, I was very good at volleyball and throwball, I soon started riding the bike for long periods.

For a year, I trained myself—twice a day. My goal was to ride the bike as fast as I could, concentrating on improving my timing. Before school, I would run for 2 kms and then cycle for about 20 kms. After I came home, I cycled again—improving my speed every day.

Bhau helped me out with my physical training, encouraging me to go further, and adding mile after mile to my programme. I practised by competing against my younger brother—the only person with whom I feel free to share my doubts and frustrations. He studies at the same school as me, and we also compete in chess—but he beats me every time!

My two older sisters encourage me whenever I take part in a cycling competition. Yugandhara has a degree in electronics and has recently started working, and Vasundhara is in the last year of mechanical engineering. Our parents gave us all a good education.

A year after I began, some coaches saw me training and, recognizing my talent, helped me plan a schedule. I was very motivated to do competitive cycling, but my dad refused to buy me a proper bike. He said that sports was the most difficult stream to get into, for, once you were in, you could not turn back. Also, a racing bicycle was far more expensive than his own bike. I understood the logic behind his thinking—cycling is a hard sport and if I did not practise enough, his money would be wasted. However, seeing how eager I was to excel in my chosen sport, and after giving me loads of advice, dad finally bought me a sort of racing bike worth ₹11,000.

At the first strike, I passed the zonal and inter-zonal races, representing our school at the state level. I won many local races, including one in Gujarat, and was among the top ten girls who competed. But my bicycle was really not that efficient, and a coach who had seen me perform told my dad that I needed a better bike to become more successful. Bhau, now satisfied that I would not quit, bought me a costlier bicycle. To me, it was the best bike ever; I trained non-stop on it.

Like cycling, life is a sport—a game—and mine started in 1998, the year I was born. In my childhood, I had no ambitions, no goals and not much money. Our family—mom, dad, my two elder sisters, my younger brother and me—lived in a noisy and crowded neighbourhood. Water was supplied to the community only twice a week and every morning there was a fight to get our share of it. In winter nights, the six of us slept in one bed, huddled together to keep each other warm, and our TV was older than my eldest sister, who is 26 years old! But our kitchen smelled delicious every day, no matter what mom cooked; our small sitting room was big enough to entertain guests. In the evenings, neighbours came over to give us news of what had happened in the community that day—just like newspapers. And at night, a girl who lived nearby told us scary ghost stories. I was born in a place of happiness.

Both my parents are schoolteachers. Aai, my mom, works with high school students; Bhau teaches classes 8 and 9. I got my determination from my dad. He has a very strict personality, and believes that every task must be done perfectly. 'To gain big,' he reminds me, 'you must work hard.' Aai is soft-hearted, a good and caring mother. She works from 4.30 a.m. to 11.30 p.m., quietly motivating me—giving me the energy to do my best. I want to be the best daughter, so that she is proud of me.

We used to live in Munjaba Vasti, a community where people were kind-hearted but not well-educated—girls were not encouraged to do higher studies or mix freely with boys, and the male child was considered 'the light of the house'! I was 9 years old when we moved to a new home in Dhanori—an army cantonment area. Unlike the rest of Pune, where buildings are coming up all the time, new development is not allowed in Dhanori. It is also a community that motivates and encourages young people to do better things.

In the rainy season, I spent my days caring for the puppies and kittens that took shelter in a shed behind our house, making sure they were fed before I ate my lunch. Every alternate day, I was given one rupee, and I filled my pockets with differently shaped toffees—small pigeons, sparrows, tigers, lions and stars. I was a playful and naughty child—running off to a cotton farm when we went to the village or hiding for hours behind the staircase at home until Aai panicked, thinking I was kidnapped or had drowned in a well!

The fire to do something different must have been in me from birth, and as I grew, the fire burned brighter. I became serious in my studies and focused on things that were difficult and would make me look clever! I tried to be like the kind doctor in our community who gave sweet tablets to kids—calcium pills, good for our bones. I was so impressed by him that my first ambition was to become a doctor.

Until Class 4, I studied in Yashwantrao Chavan Vidyaniketan, the first English-medium government school in Pune. From the beginning, I noticed the unfair practices in the school—teachers gave extra attention to their favourite students, the 'special ones' were allowed to cheat during exam time, while the rest of us were punished if even a small part of our homework was not completed. Seeing this unfairness my wish to become a doctor disappeared; I was determined to stay put in this school to bring improvements in its educational system.

But God had another gift waiting for me. I got admission and a scholarship to the Akanksha K.C. Thackeray Vidya Niketan (KCTVN), a well-known school in Pune. Not wanting to leave my present school until I had made the changes I wanted to, I did not inform my parents of this new opportunity. But the new school telephoned my dad; I was forced to drop out before I could make any improvements in my school.

KCTVN English-medium school was a different world. It had brilliant teachers who treasured every student. I had this theory that school meant only studying from books. But KCTVN had completely opposite ideas. Here, we had to understand what we learnt and not just mug up for the exams. The ideas, environment, faces—everything was new. But the first three months were a nightmare. I could not understand the different methods of teaching—my confidence began to slip. I grew quieter, felt lonely and was becoming a failure. At night, I cried... I could not digest these changes in my life. It took me a year to come out of my shell. It was my class teacher, Prashant Sir, who showed me how to study, solve problems and participate in class activities, and slowly the dark clouds passed away.

Today, I am happy to have these not-so-good memories, because they made my later enjoyment of the school even sweeter. For this was the school that helped me build values, developed my personality and realized my dreams. It taught me to fight for the right things, in the right way. KCTVN was my Hogwarts school!

The first award I received—a certificate for 100 per cent attendance—motivated me and gave me a thirst for recognition. I started collecting trophies in drawing, leadership skills, science and technology, and later in athletics, throwball and volleyball. With each award, my competitive spirit grew and I regained my earlier confidence. I started to love school more than anything else. I reached school as early as possible, took part in all activities and was attentive in classes, where, earlier, I had hardly been awake.

Our didis and bhaiyas became our family members and mentors; Kanchan Didi and Manoj Bhaiya gave me a good foundation in English and maths, and I began to enjoy both the subjects. God made me a lucky person to have friends like Triveni, who helped me with my problems. Foreigners came to teach us for short periods—their English accents fascinated me, and when I heard how confidently they spoke I would get goosebumps! I learnt from everyone and from everywhere, and that is what has made me who I am today.

My cycling career took off in my tenth year in school. There is a struggle in all riders before they cross the winning line, but the joy of victory pushes us on. I loved the feeling of riding against the wind, dusting myself after a fall and getting back onto the bike to ride again—maybe to win. Just for fun, I took part in the state-level trials held in Pune, and was surprised to be selected as the fourth rider in the national-level team. Later, I was given a fixed position in the Maharashtra Cycling Team—this honour inspired me to face tougher challenges.

On my seventeenth birthday, Bhau got me a one-of-a-kind, second-hand bike. She was beautiful. Her previous owner must have thought so too, because she was in a very good condition. I fell in love with her instantly—she fitted me perfectly. Now she goes with me everywhere and we have a good relationship. All my bikes have names—Blue Storm, Red Queen and Black Fury. Often, when I feel bored or disheartened, I find myself talking to them, especially during race time. They are my friends; I can trust them no matter what.

In the final Class 10, Secondary School Certificate (SSC) exam, I secured 80 per cent—a distinction—and the same year I won my first national bronze medal. I was so happy, it felt like Holi and Diwali had come together! I wanted to continue studies in science or medicine and keep cycling—both at my very best levels.

Aai always wanted me to become a doctor, and was happy that I was trying to pursue a sport as well as science, but Bhau felt differently. He was not against my cycling or studying to be a doctor, but he said that if I tried to do both, I would not succeed in either. Science was a difficult subject in the Higher Secondary Certificate (HSC) board, and Bhau insisted that science and my cycling routine could not go hand-in-hand. It was like a gun put to my head! In the end, the problem got solved because the medical colleges in Pune were too costly, and I did not meet their admission requirements.

I took Arts to study psychology, which is also a science. Maybe one day I will change my path and study medicine. After six months in Class 11, I was certain that following two careers, though risky, was not an impossible task. I passed my HSC Class 12 exam with a first class and was selected for the National Games in Kerala. Yes! I had proved to Bhau that sports and studies can go together.

There was more excitement ahead of me—the National Games! They happen every two years and only senior cyclists can participate in them. In 2015 I was selected to take part—the youngest rider in the Maharashtra Team! This was a sparkling star in my sports career, and I was grateful to bring pride to my family, teachers and the Sir of the Maharashtra Cycling Association who gave me the opportunity to represent the state.

A professional cyclist can get lonely—this is especially true in times of defeat. Just the thought that I have disappointed many people makes me feel lonely and depressed. I also feel lonely when I am fighting for something that everyone else opposes. Lance Armstrong has been a role model. The determination and struggles described in his book, *It's Not About the Bike: My Journey Back to Life*, have inspired me to train harder. Anna Meares, Marianne Vos and Wai Sze Lee are world record holders in cycling; I would love to be like them—strong in every way.

I am now in first year (BA) at Baburaoji Gholap College, Sangvi, in Pune. While studying for HSC, I realized that good time management made the difference between people who achieve success and the many who could have, but don't. I divide my time between the many things that need to be done. My daily routine starts much before college begins. After waking up at 4.30 a.m., I do stretching exercises, go for a 5-km run, have a quick breakfast, practise cycling for three hours, returning home at 8.30 a.m. before going to college. Evenings are spent in strength training. It is important to focus on my weaknesses—riding up hills, doing sprints, leading the group. At every session I push myself to do better. But for god's sake, how boring life would be if I had been born perfect!

We need to experience all the colours of life—to know black we must be able to see white. If we never fail, we can never be successful. I think people don't really fear hard work—they fear the failure that might come at the end of it. That is why they sit idle and don't try hard enough to succeed. Luckily, my love for success is greater than my fear of failure. We are all heroes. Only a few people recognize this, for, most of us do not believe that the magic is within us. The saying, 'We are powerful beyond the magic', is proved by many success stories. I hope my story will be one of them.

A professional cyclist, like everyone else, faces pressures. Many quit, while some get stuck in pit-holes longer than others. When things don't work, I try to analyse what went wrong, and give myself time to come out of the situation. I remind myself that I can be the best—if things aren't working out, it's just because I'm taking the day off!

There is still a lot to learn; I learn from anyone who shares knowledge with me. Besides technical cycling skills, I must develop self-confidence, self-knowledge, self-discipline, patience and determination—all the steps needed to reach my goal of representing India in the Olympics. Inside me, and in front of me, there is a new flame of fire. I am going to train for the Tokyo Olympics in 2020. I have already started cycling... towards the Olympic flame.

∽

'We are all heroes. Only a few people recognize this, most of us do not believe that the magic is within us.'

JYOTI REDDY | AKANKSHA | 1998 TO 2008
BA, Sociology and Anthropology, St Xavier's College, Mumbai
Communications Manager, *Education World: The Human Development Magazine*
Date of Birth: 9 October 1993

MY FATHER'S DAUGHTER

I was 9 years old when I first held a camera; I felt like a princess with a mighty sword. Kaushal Parikh, a photographer, had come to the Akanksha Centre in Mumbai to take pictures of us—candid shots he called them. My curious eyes followed him wherever he went. The camera fascinated me and I tagged along Bhaiya, nagging him to show me the images each time he clicked. This fascination with photography has stayed with me.

I was 13 when Abba, my father, passed away. Most fathers prayed for a male child, mine, was super elated when he had a daughter. I idolized my dad; he was my best friend. We joked and hung out together in the park, talking about everything—my problems, his childhood, even his first wife. Abba gave me a sense of comfort, a freedom that never restricted me in any way. My girlfriends found this unusual, because they were scared of their fathers and could never talk to them freely.

As I was growing up, Abba told me stories—not of pretty princesses, but of women warriors who had done extraordinary things in life. He wanted me to be brave and independent, even though our community did not accept girls who wanted to do things their own way—the free-thinking girls. He made me believe I was not bound by anything, that I could be anything—an astronaut, a painter, a film-maker or a storyteller. Abba meant the world to me, and when I lost him, I was pushed out of my comfort zone.

My father died of TB but I hysterically blamed Amma for not looking after him better. Sitting in a corner at the Akanksha Centre with Anjali Didi, I vented out the feelings inside me. Like with Abba, I had a two-way relationship with Didi—she knew everything about me and I knew everything about her. I did not understand then my mother's grief, or that being a working woman with three children to support (she was a helper at the Akanksha Centre), she just had too little time to comfort me.

Around the same time, a documentary film-maker from the UK came to the Centre to teach us the process of making personal video diaries. We were each given a camera and were free to shoot anything we wanted. For a long time I was in denial and did not really accept Abba's death. I thought that maybe if I made a video diary on him, it would sort of bring him back. I decided to tell the story of my father.

I revisited all the places that we had been together, places that still held the aroma of our memories; through the making of the film I relived Abba's life and expressed my deep sadness at his death. My mother, who had, for years, been accumulating her own sorrow, pretending not to miss him, was in tears when she saw the video.

The emotional effect my father's video had on Amma and me made me think...that the joys and problems of people around me were not different from those in the world of cinema, and everyone wants a happy ending! Stories carry strong messages, films make the greatest impact—I decided to be a film-maker.

It was Abba who inspired me to pursue my passion. His love for cooking had made him get into the catering business. The money he earned as a head chef was just about okay for us to survive and mom kept nagging him to get a better job. I remember his promise, 'I will take care of you, but at no cost give up my cooking. In a different job, I will never find this kind of happiness; if I am not happy, I cannot make the family happy.' Today I understand what he meant.

The first twelve years of my life were the best ones. I was extremely lucky to have parents who wanted to educate their children. My friends, who are better off than me, aren't awed by this, for educational opportunities are a norm in their society. I grew up in a reality where girls did not go college—they were often married before they reached puberty. For many, it was also an escape from the strict conditions in their own homes.

Abba's childhood was a difficult one; he grew up on the streets of Mumbai from the age of 4. When he was 8, his father passed away, leaving him to be raised by a woman from a Muslim family. We call her Phupi and are still in touch with her.

Born a Hindu and brought up a Muslim, my dad diligently followed both Hinduism and Islam. After he married my mom, a Christian, we observed the rituals of all three religions. Abba believed in humanity, and when I questioned the existence of only one God, he told me to follow the path that made sense to me—making me responsible for my own choices. Friends in the community were very surprised; they were never asked for their opinions nor had the freedom to make decisions.

I was Abba's favourite, the pampered one, but he was generous with all of us—at every festival he bought new clothes for Mama and his children. Sometimes, I would crib that I didn't have nice clothes to wear for a friend's birthday party, until the day I opened Abba's trunk—he had only two pairs of clothes in it! Seeing the sacrifices he made for his family, I felt guilty and selfish. He never complained, he loved unconditionally and selflessly.

Our home was on a main road—one room made of sheets of corrugated tin and plastic. Like architects, Abba and I did renovations to make it more comfortable to live in. Very early in life, I learnt to be content with the limited resources we had—one bucket of water was enough for three of us to bathe! There were struggles but we just never looked at them that way.

Although our home was basic, it came as a shock when it was demolished by the BMC. We were 'rehabilitated' from our city slum, to a solid cement building in Mankhurd—a suburb we had never heard of. Our new room did not leak during the rainy months, nor like before did we need to 'steal' electricity from different lines to light our bulbs. Three taps were allotted to each flat and it was a huge relief to have a water supply, even though it was not regular. We now had the basic necessities for everyday living.

However, the new home in Mankhurd brought new problems. It was surrounded by slums that had been in the area for many years. Groups of young men from the slums would enter our compound with knives and swords, threatening and brutally beating up our boys. Eve-teasing, molestation, bad language, rapes and even murders became common. Stricter restrictions were imposed on girls, as parents worried about our safety. But this dangerous situation had a positive side—the bonds between members of our community became stronger. Perhaps, one day, I will make a film with the stories I have collected in our new environment.

My formal learning began in a municipal school where teachers had no expectations from students; we were pushed from one class to a higher one without being taught anything! That was the way the system worked. We simply went to school for free meals and to have fun with friends. After the school day ended, I went to an evening centre run by Akanksha, an NGO. Here, I was given opportunities to discover different aspects of myself. Me—the dancer, poet, photographer and storyteller.

Anjali Didi, seeing that I had potential, got me transferred to Class 9 in Little Flower of Jesus High School, a private school where I was required to think for myself, to explore on my own. It was difficult for me to adjust to this new way of learning, and, failing twice in a row, I lost my confidence and refused to sit in the same class for the third time with classmates younger than me. But at no cost would Didi allow me to give up. She prodded me, 'I know you can do it, I know you can do it.' Her belief in me pushed me to give it another try and it finally brought results. I graduated as the Head Girl of my school.

At the Centre I met students from the elite Cathedral School. They came with preconceived notions about slum kids, but Anjali Didi treated us all the same, and soon we were working together—on presentations, debates, the Model United Nations project (I represented Luxembourg) and the annual Akanksha event. In time, friendships between us were defined by our respect for each other, not by our different backgrounds. Sahir and Akash, both Cathedralites, became good friends. Today, Sahir is in the US, but Akash and I meet whenever our busy work schedules allow us to.

During these years Amma had been borrowing money to meet our expenses, and when she could not pay back in time, she was humiliated by the moneylenders. To stop this borrowing, I decided to quit studies and start working. Once again, Anjali Didi firmly stood her ground, saying there was no way I could give up school.

Together we figured out part-time jobs that would also give me time to study. I was only 14 years old but had matured at an early age. I worked as a ticket collector at a theatre box office, taught in a playgroup school, organized kids' parties and interned at Teach for India (TFI) and Ogilvy & Mather.

Amma's pride in my academic achievements encouraged me to study harder. Getting admission into St Xavier's Junior College not only boosted my confidence, but also gave me space to explore without limitations—pushing me to know myself better. I never let my circumstances hinder my learning. Most students in college were dressed way better than me and carried fancy gadgets to class, but when one of my professors reassured me that I was at par with the other students—as smart and dumb as any of them—I giggled and felt much better. The professor was right. Today, I hold a degree in sociology and anthropology—the first graduate in my family—and my peers, unaware of my lower economic background, appreciate me for who I am.

There are many things that interest me—documentary films, religion, world cultures, international relations, photography and anthropology. Once I find out exactly what I want to do, I would like to go abroad for my postgraduate degree.

In 2015, Sangeeta, an Akanksha alumnus, founded Prayatna, an initiative to get kids to take action to develop their community. Our working team of Akanksha alumni and local residents conducted clean-up drives, visiting eighty-two households to make them aware of the negative impact of accumulated garbage on the health of their community. The biggest hurdle we faced was the attitude of the adults—they had become immune to the filth they lived in! So, Jeesu Mandumpal and I focused on the new generation—the kids in the community.

The classes begin at 6.30 a.m. on Sundays! We show short films and commercials, organize talks and discussions on cleanliness, gender stereotyping, early marriages, leadership and happiness. Children are also exposed to TV programmes that offer them more suitable content than the serials they watch! Books are an essential part of these Sunday classes; the Art and Design workshop with Anand Bhaiya encourages the children to find the artist in themselves.

Our kids now see things with different perspectives; they look for beauty around them. Yes, my students are my gems— my best friends, and my teachers too. When I correct them for not doing homework, or for copying stories from TV cartoons instead of creating their own, they are quick to point out my flaws, but surprisingly they still tell me that I am perfect!

I have often been referred to as 'underprivileged'. It never used to bother me earlier, but now, I cannot digest that term! Privileged, is a label that puts one into a particular slot in society. I am from a low-income family, but I am privileged compared to my friends who are already married, to my mother who was abandoned as a child and had to eat from dustbins to kill her hunger, to those who never had the opportunity to go to college like I did. Many of my community friends are privileged too—some will be dancers, entrepreneurs, teachers and beauty specialists. We are certainly not underprivileged!

My desire to tell stories through the medium of video and film has only grown stronger. In 2015, I got a job as an assistant in a production house, but it did not work out. I wanted my lens to capture the lives of people; the company only made ads for products I didn't believe in! I stuck around for about a year to get experience in the art and logistics of film-making.

I am now a Communications Manager with *Education World: The Human Development Magazine*, making documentaries for schools and NGOs all over the country, doing what I love the best—making films. In the long term, I wish to start my own company, travel and collect stories for films that will contribute to world peace and happiness. And then much later in life, I will sit down and narrate these same stories to my grandchildren! But first, I must explore myself—be lost somewhere, to find the true me.

Perhaps, the greatest thing that Abba taught me was to listen to my heart. Borrowing a line from a film of his favourite actor, Rajesh Khanna, he would say, '*Kuch to log kahenge, logon ka kam hai kehna*' (people will talk, that is what they like to do). He did not listen to others, only to his heart. His life was short, but happy. I, too, will never be happy by only making money. What matters more, much more, is never taking the smile off one's face!

Abba used to tell me to keep a treasure box to store all my happiness, 'Collect the little things that make you happy,' he advised, 'that way you can have many of them.' With a smile that reaches my eyes, I look back on all the pieces of happiness I have collected—eating a ₹10 dish of sweet firni at Mohammed Ali Road, posing for a photo on the swing in the public garden, Mama's joy when I became the Head Girl in school, my relief when the professor said I was as good or as bad as any college student. I am learning to find happiness in whatever I do.

My brother, Anand, who is three years younger to me, left college in his first year to support the family and now works in the Human Resources Department of the Future Group. Sagar, six years younger to me, is in junior college, and plans to get into a self-designed learning programme at Swaraj University, Udaipur.

I hear Abba's voice, 'Jyoti, always be there for your Amma and brothers. You are a reflection of me.' He has given me a huge responsibility. Whenever I am disheartened and don't know what to do, I write a letter to Abba, and keep it under my pillow. Then, I think of what he would have done in my situation—and I do just that.

∽

'Abba used to tell me to keep a treasure box to store all my happiness. "Collect the little things that make you happy," he advised, "that way you can have many of them."'

YOGESH CHAURE | AKANKSHA | 2005 TO 2016
Junior College, KV B.E.G. College, Pune
Poet and Blogger
Date of Birth: 29 June 1999

SAYING IT IN VERSE

Surely I'll miss my older days
But now I have to find new ways
Because to make a difference
I must change
Myself before anything else
And this journey is a lonely one
There will be cold winters
And a tyrant sun
But to make a difference
I must change
Myself before anything else
YOGESH CHUARE

Writing poetry has given me a way to think about the changes I need to make in my life. I started writing while waiting for the results of my Class 10 board examinations. Until Class 7, I was the top of my batch; after that things went downhill and my scores were terrible. If my final results were not good, my future was doomed.

Arrogant, rude and distracted in class, I had a bad reputation in school, and after failing for two consecutive years my behaviour had got worse. My mother and the didis and bhaiyas at Akanksha were disappointed in me. The board results were to be announced a month after the last test paper; and with each day of waiting, my guilt and fear of failure grew. I desperately wanted to alter the course of my life, but was it already too late? All the quotations I had read on how to succeed had not helped my poor attitude or work habits.

With time on my hands after the exams, I would surf the Internet and read different blogs, and also started one of my own at wordpress.com. My first few articles were on climate change, atheism and supporting the lesbian, gay, bisexual and transgender (LGBT) community—three subjects that interest me. There is a grave danger to our planet, unless we take steps to lessen global warming; I am suspicious of those who try to deny this. To me, religion is only a basic set of rules, which, if not followed, wrongly condemn us or make us feel guilty. An example is the fourteenth-century astronomer, Nicolaus Copernicus, who discovered that the earth revolved around the sun, and was put into solitary confinement because the church opposed his discovery. I also don't believe that it is a crime to love someone of your own kind.

On my blog, I expressed some of these feelings:

Oh speakers of God
Tell me something about
How your God must have
Made me as I am
Is it his mistake or is it mine
That I am in love with my own kind
Should I let it go
Or keep it inside
Should I just be
What you want
And keep pretending what I'm not

I read poems of other bloggers—Vincent Mars at The Boy with a Hat and Melody's on betrayal at Thoughts: muffled bones & poetry. Becoming adventurous, I experimented with my own poems. The first responses were encouraging and I continued writing. Blogging made the period of waiting for my exam results pass away quickly; I became calmer and less depressed.

When the examination results were announced, I had scored 70 per cent! It was one of the happiest days of my life. My mother was delighted, but sadly my father could not celebrate with us—he had died seven years ago.

Ana, my father, had had a hard life. My grandfather, a bailiff in Pune district, had little time for his son, and father got into bad company, dropped out of school and ended up as an autorickshaw driver, working ten hours every day for the rest of his life. Every Saturday and Sunday, he would take me to the zoo or the park, and was very protective of me. Maybe that's why I loved him so much. I was 4 or 5 years old when he left my mother for another woman. But, every week I would go and stay with him for three days; and whenever he had time, we would drive around the city in his autorickshaw, with me sitting next to him on the driver's seat. He was an average-looking man with a good heart, and even when he left home, he gave my mother money to raise me.

Mother was a scrap collector. Each morning, with other scrap pickers, she took the train to the hill station of Lonavala and left my brother, Mangesh, to look after me. Mangesh was passionate about cricket, and I used to sit near the 'cricket pitch' and watch him play. He made sure I did not get into trouble, keeping me off the street, feeding me whenever I was hungry and protecting me from the bigger kids. Unfortunately, he didn't finish school and works as a security guard. We are still close to each other.

My education began in a Marathi-medium Pune Municipal Corporation (PMC) school where I spent most of the time playing and bunking classes. The teachers were often absent, so not much work was done in the classroom and the syllabus lagged behind. When the teachers did come, they were irritable, and if we did not behave, they beat us with sticks or rulers.

Ana died when I was in Class 4 and my world stopped. I could not even attend his funeral because his second wife informed us only two weeks after his death. I missed him terribly. No longer interested in playing with friends or bunking school, I spent time alone—crying for hours. My routine changed completely—I began to concentrate on my studies, stopped skipping classes and topped my batch in Class 8.

It was Vimal Mausi, a neighbour, who took me to the Akanksha Centre. Seeing me wasting my time after school— playing marbles, roaming on the streets, getting into trouble— Mausi decided that I should be doing something more useful! I was only 5 years old, but was excited to go to this new place. Together with some of my friends, I got into a line, and a tall man, Santosh Bhaiya, called out our names. After the roll call, we were taken to a small and peaceful bungalow—not like our home which was always filled with noise! The class started with a simple prayer, and for two hours, we did interesting activities. The Centre had a warm and nice feeling.

The PMC school ended at Class 7, and after passing the entrance test, I got admission into a Kendriya Vidyalaya (KV), a central government institution. The KV schools have a good reputation, and I was very lucky that Mrs Anu Aga, one of Akanksha's Board members, offered me a seat from her Rajya Sabha quota. The medium of instruction in KV was English, the kids were disciplined and the teachers came to class regularly.

It was very different, much better than my earlier school; but, having only studied in Marathi, I continued to think in Marathi, and it was difficult to change over to English.

The teachers helped me as much as they could, but the studious kids did not accept me, and being too proud to ask for their help, I became lazy, hanging out with the most-reluctant-to study kids—the school goons. They were tough and I had a small built, so my friendship with them also gave me physical protection! Teachers complained that I never studied or completed my classwork; I could hardly finish a maths test! My grades slipped, but I managed to pass Class 8—with very low marks.

Thinking about Akanksha's generous scholarship, and the sacrifices my mother had made to give me a good education, hurt my conscience. But my desire to improve would immediately be followed by doubt—was it possible to change my bad habits? In Class 9, my marks got even worse, and in the final examination, I failed in maths, and was not promoted to the next class.

Mother, who was until now under the impression that I was working hard and doing well in school, was totally shocked when I failed. I hated myself. But there was some hope—if I passed a supplementary exam, I could still be promoted. The exam was in seventeen days; I had one year's syllabus to study. At this crucial point, God sent Manoj Bhaiya into my life. Bhaiya is a simple guy with a good sense of humour, and, best of all, he is brilliant at maths. Even though I had no basic understanding of the subject and had become lazy over the years, Bhaiya managed to make me study. I went into the first exam literally shaking with nervousness, but after a quick look at the question paper, I sighed with relief and confidently answered the questions. The results were declared three days later—I had passed.

After Class 10, I was done with maths! I am now in KV Beg College, Pune, studying Humanities—political theory, history and geography—but my favourite subject is history. Socially, college is difficult. Not being an extrovert, I have few friends. Bhargavi, my only friend in college, reads my poetry but most of the other students think I am peculiar. Having spent a large part of my childhood in a fantasy world with aliens and other imaginary creatures, maybe I am different! Badass characters like Artemis Fowl from a book by Eoin Colfer, and Severus Snape, the half-blood prince in J.K. Rowling's books have always attracted me. I get bored reading about the goody-goodys.

Living in a crowded community with 24x7 activity, continual loud noises, and having five people packed into our small house, made it difficult to study at home. So the time I am not in college, is spent at the Akanksha office, sitting next to Manoj Bhaiya's computer table. It is a good place to study, and Bhaiya is right there when I need him.

Many different roads lie before me, but Azim Premji University (APU) in Bengaluru, a premier institution, is a first option. I plan to crack the entrance test and after APU, specialize in literature and teach in a college. My love for travel has been influenced by the TV channel, Fox Traveller, and the programme, *Eat Street*, has made me curious to taste exotic foods. With travel journalism, I can earn a living and fulfil my passion to see the world. Another exciting career possibility is mass media or perhaps I will end up studying communication skills. A career in design is also a possibility. The National Institute of Design in Ahmedabad, and other institutes in Bengaluru and Mumbai have fascinating courses, and maybe I will end up studying TV animation. The long-term goal is to go abroad to get a Master's degree in the field of study I have chosen.

These are just ideas in my head; I don't know which ones will work out. My true love remains writing and comments from other bloggers (I get ten to twelve hits daily) confirm that my poems and articles are getting better. However, I must start contributing towards family expenses and writing may not give me a steady income.

Whatever I do, like Robert Frost, I will take the road less travelled—I want to live fully.

∞

I don't wanna live in a mundane way
And I don't believe in what they say
For I must enjoy my life's thrills
Because I'm not born just to pay my bills
Life should be adventurous
Life should be fun
And I'm not part of
That materialistic run
As money and fame is just a part
But I wanna live as my heart
Tells me to do and say
And I love to live this way
Because my life should be full of thrills
And I'm not born just to pay my bills

SUMEET GADE | AKANKSHA | 1996 TO 2005
BA, Dr T.K. Tope Arts and Commerce Night College, Mumbai
Community Engagement Associate, Teach For India
Founder, Pragati Holistic Development Trust
Date of Birth: 27 December 1987

BRIDGING TWO WORLDS

Soon after my birth I got severe jaundice. When the doctors said I may not make it, Dadaji (grandfather) refused to pay the hospital charges—he did not want to waste his money! My father never came to the hospital; it was only my mother's faith that kept me alive.

Father was a big-time alcoholic. People would direct us to the different spots in our locality where he had fallen, drunk and asleep—'*Tera baap idhar pada hai, udhar pada hai*' (your father has fallen down here, fallen down there). Many times, Mummy and I pulled him out of garbage bins. At first, I was too young to know why he kept collapsing, but after a while even I knew he was addicted to alcohol. He used to come home completely drunk and beat my mother, brother and me, throwing things at us until late at night. Every single day, I saw my mother crying and being abused. It was particularly bad when he needed money to buy his liquor, for, then he threw us out of the house. Those days were like hell.

Father must have spent most of his salary on alcohol, because even though he had a job as a watchman at the Mahalaxmi Racecourse in Mumbai, we were always very poor. There were days when there was no money to buy dal and we only ate rice mixed with water. But Mummy stayed hopeful, and with tears in her eyes she would promise, 'Today the dal got over, next time we will eat nice food.' Most nights there was no rice or dal; we went to bed after eating Parle-G biscuits. I think she suffered the most, feeling completely helpless to protect her children.

I was brought up in a rigid Maharashtrian family where education was not a big concern, and not being able to afford the fees, I dropped out in Class 1. When I went to my Dadaji for advice, he picked me up and banged me against the wall. His words still haunt me, *'Tera baap sharabi hai, tu padh likh kar kya karega? Mera paisa hai, tere baap ka nahi, bada hokar kya banega? Tere baap jaisa hi banega na, to kyun padhna hai?'* (Your father is an alcoholic, what are you going to achieve by studying? This is my money, not your father's. What will you be when you grow up except be like your father, then what's the use of studying?)

After that visit to Dadaji, there was another awful experience. My father threatened to throw my brother and me from the fifth floor of a building if he was not given money to buy his drinks. My mother, desperate to save us, ran out to sell her gold mangalsutra. The mangalsutra saved us, but Mummy was humiliated. She had been forced to sell the most holy symbol of her Hindu marriage. After that, we went to live with my Nana and Nani (maternal grandparents), and never returned home. I saw my father again only three or four times, and then many years later went to his funeral.

I don't remember calling my father Dad or Baba—maybe I have forgotten, or maybe I didn't call him anything. My Nana filed an FIR at the police station, and for a year I went regularly from school to court, to give evidence of my father's physical abuse. Each time we went, as is usual in Indian courts—*'tareekh par tareekh milti gai'*—the case was postponed from one date to another. In the end, my father got a strict warning and was let off. The FIR papers neatly piled in our house remind me of the nightmares I had—standing in front of the judge with a packet of Parle-G biscuits in my hand.

For more than twenty years we have lived with our Nana and Nani. Nani—always smiling—is illiterate but is an active community worker. Nana is a content and generous man. Whenever he has extra money, he buys us new clothes, happy to wear torn shirts himself. Everything good that I have done was inspired by my grandparents.

Even though Nani's home was filled with love and kindness, I became arrogant, and every argument ended up in a fight. Why did I behave this way? Only now do I know the answer. I was following in the footsteps of the father I hated. Doing exactly what he did—using my fists to get what I wanted. I had changed homes; but it was much more difficult to change myself. My reputation in the community was bad but I didn't care.

I had friends—a group of boys who met every day to play cricket before afternoon school. One morning, no one showed up and this continued for a whole week! I looked all over the slum for my gang, and finally found them in a house with a social worker who was talking about hygiene, nutrition and good habits. I was shocked. Why waste time with hygiene classes instead of playing cricket? The social worker was from Akanksha, an NGO I had never heard of, but the woman invited me to join the class. No stranger had ever been interested in me before—I was suspicious, but curious.

The next day I was in the class by 9 a.m. and the room was already overcrowded. The first session was about good eating habits, '*Sprouts khana chahiye, teen time meal lena chahiye*' (you should eat sprouts and have meals thrice a day). What was she talking about? *Yahan ek time khane ko nahi milta, aap teen time meal khane ko keh rahe ho* (Here we don't even get one meal, and you're telling us to eat three times a day!) I was like—*ye shabd bol bachchan hain* (this is just hot air talk!)

After the session, we were each given a banana—a clever strategy to keep the kids coming back! I started attending the class to get the banana! The social worker's name was Kavita Didi and I was 9 years old when she enrolled me in the Mahalaxmi Akanksha Centre. I felt loved and important, just like in my Nani's home. Didi and I became good friends and later I escorted other didis through the slums, picking up children who were absent from class and helping to develop relationships with the community.

The semi-private Marathi-medium school I went to ran on donations provided by Christian missionaries, and since I was a single-parent child, they waived half my fees. I was an average student with no ambition. My English scores were higher than Marathi—my mother tongue—because we only spoke in English at Akanksha. But the rest of my studies were suffering and I was often sent to the last bench in the classroom. I had a bad image of myself, certain I would do nothing special in my life.

My maths teacher at school constantly made fun of my mistakes and threw me out of class. By God's grace, and the BMC rules that did not allow any student to fail, I reached Class 10. During the maths preliminary tests, the Maths Sir came up to me and said, 'Sumeet, you're a good-for-nothing fellow. If you pass this paper, I will distribute 50 kilos of pedas (sweetmeats) in school.' I failed the test, getting a zero in one paper and a miserable two marks in the other; Sir saved his money—he did not have to distribute the pedas! Since this was my first attempt at the exam, I was not discouraged, 'OK, *theek hai, chal jata hai*' (that's okay, no big deal.)

I reappeared for the exam twice and failed both times. Stress built up, my self-esteem was zero, my confidence went for a toss. Maths had made my life hell. I was tagged a failure, a good-for-nothing. Life is result-oriented and I could not produce the results! I stopped going to Akanksha and meeting friends. My uncle would nag me, '*Sab free mein milta hai, jao, kaam karo aur khao*' (you get everything for free, go to work, earn something, and then you can eat). So I took any job I could find—loading and unloading trucks at the racecourse, lining up horses for the Gymkhana races, even shouting slogans at political rallies.

Everything depended upon getting a piece of paper—a Class 10 certificate, and I could just not get it. Before my fourth attempt at the exam, I decided to commit suicide. I ran away from home and took sleeping pills. But, after a nice long sleep, I woke up the next day feeling just fine! I tried again, this time by cutting my veins, but that too didn't work. My plan had failed, I could not even commit suicide!

At the Akanksha Centre, Rajshree Didi and Dev Bhaiya noticed that I was skipping classes, my work was deteriorating and I was depressed. Didi slowly rebuilt my confidence—she never said I was a failure; she tried to figure out what was going on in my head, visited my home to understand our family situation, spent time with me after classes and took me out to dinner. She sent me to a counsellor, Dr Pervin Dadachanji— the best of the best. I was given medication and I felt better, but later discovered that it was only a placebo to build my self-esteem! Rajshree Didi's belief that every child is basically good gave me confidence that I could change myself.

In my fourth attempt, I cleared the exams, thanks to Dev Bhaiya who tutored me in maths. After this, I never looked back. I shared my success story at a parents' meeting and this changed the game. I had become a winner and one success followed another. My new job was 'shadowing' Bhaiya—introducing him to families in the community, helping him solve their problems. I earned ₹1,000 a month, and after keeping ₹300 for travelling expenses, I gave the rest to my mother. One month, I did something I had always wanted to do—I invited Rajshree Didi to a restaurant and spent my entire month's salary on the dinner!

I have completed a BA degree at the Dr T.K. Tope Night College, and want to enrol for an MBA or a Master's degree in Social Entrepreneurship. I just need to figure out how and where I can get a scholarship. After that, I will travel abroad to study further, and get work experience, for, in this global world, it is necessary to think big—bigger than India.

Akanksha's SLP was started in 2004 to create a space for those who were interested in making a career in social work. I was one of SLP's first batch of students. Each student's potential was identified and a programme was designed for them. In SLP, we discussed local and global issues in history, current affairs, geography and also focused on adolescent anxieties. I enjoyed SLP, did extremely well in it and developed leadership qualities.

The programme encouraged us to look further than ourselves, and at the end of the course my friends and I founded an NGO called Pragati Holistic Development Trust. The aim of the Trust is to interact with hospitalized children, give them a good time and support them in every way we can. I have learnt so much from these kids. Many are seriously ill but still put up a brave fight. I feel ashamed of myself when I think of the time when I tried to end my life, even though I had many more options than these children. Spending time at the hospital and making the kids happy, makes me happy too. In 2009, we got registered as a charitable trust and, so far, have supported 6,000 kids. There are thousands more who need our help. I am determined to take Pragati to different parts of Maharashtra and other states in India.

The values I saw being practised at Akanksha have become a part of me. I now respect people and am no longer suspicious of them. I see the plus side of being honest and am positive in difficult situations. Sometimes I wonder how this all happened? Was it the respect of the teachers who never bothered that I was from a scheduled caste? The freedom I had at the Centre to learn at my own pace? The self-worth that I discovered in myself? Perhaps it was all of these things. At Akanksha, I never felt I was a 'sharabi ka bachcha' (son of a drunkard).

In April 2013, I interviewed for a job with TFI. It was not an easy entry. I cleared multiple interviews and finally won the position—Community Engagement Associate at TFI. I had qualified on my own merit and this makes me thankful and proud. The most exciting part is that the didis and bhaiyas who taught me are now my working partners. My job is to develop processes and solutions so that TFI Fellows can interact effectively with children and adults living in slum communities. I also work directly with parents and children in TFI schools. Building a strong network between TFI and other NGOs is crucial; I am developing a system where NGOs share good practices and learn from each other's mistakes.

Accompanying a PhD student from Vienna, Austria, I have conducted surveys in the Dharavi slum community and we have given a presentation on Social Change at a youth conference in Hong Kong. In 2016, I was a participant at the Young Connectors of the Future—a programme organized by the Swedish Institute.

There are countless Sumeets in India. I want to be the bhaiya, the role model who inspires them. Young men and women in rural districts don't have educational and vocational opportunities and are bought over by power-hungry politicians and landlords, who use them to achieve their own ambitions. We must balance this negative trend. In my spare time, I do research work on NGOs in rural towns and analyse the impact of their methods of work. Five years down the line, I see myself farming and running Pragati in a rural set-up.

This is my first attempt to write my story. When I am invited to share my experiences in schools, I echo the words of my didis and bhaiyas, 'You can do anything you want to do. You can be anyone you want to be. You just have to want it enough, and do what it takes to get it.' Some of my community friends have regular jobs and no longer waste their time in drinking and gambling. My brother completed his Master's degree in marketing and is currently working with B.D. Dhalla Pvt Ltd, a transport organization in Mumbai. I like to think that my achievements inspired them.

A few years ago, I made an advance payment to buy a flat in Mumbai. We cannot move in yet because a big part of the savings was spent on medical treatment of my mother, who had multiple-organ failure. Rajshree Didi, on the advice of Dr Bela Doctor, Akanksha's caring doctor, admitted her to the ICU at Jaslok Hospital. Thank God, my mother recovered. Didi advised me to borrow the money from her and keep my savings. But I followed the values Didi had taught me and not her advice. This was my responsibility and responsibilities must be met.

The flat is in a nice concrete building, twenty minutes away from the railway station. It is registered in my mother's name and will be my gift to her. But my dream house is in Badlapur—in a compound with gardens and a swimming pool, not too far from Mumbai. I have already paid a deposit and it will be completed soon. This will be our family home, the home that we never imagined we would own.

The bad phase in my life has gone. My Nana and Nani, my mother, Rajshree Didi, Dev Bhaiya and a few others—a limited number of people have given me unlimited new ways to lead my life. I could not have done it alone.

∞

'In April 2013, I interviewed for a job with Teach For India. It was not easy. I cleared multiple interviews and finally won the position—Community Engagement Associate at TFI! I had qualified on my own merit and this makes me thankful and proud.'

REVATI CHANDRASHEKHAR POTE | AKANKSHA | 2007 TO 2015

Student, Maharashtra Institute of Technology Polytechnic, Pune

Founder, We Are Change, an NGO

Date of Birth: 7 November 1999

NO ORDINARY SCHOOL

My father drives a rented autorickshaw and my mother is a teacher. I am equally proud of both of them. Mama had given the Class 10 board examination soon after they were married and Papa encouraged her to continue her studies. Today, she is a graduate and teaches in Suprabhat, an independent NGO, under the umbrella of a well-known organization called Pratham. She hopes to do her MA too.

In India's chauvinistic society, most men would never permit their female partners to be more educated than them, but my father is an exception. He works approximately ten to twelve hours a day and earns ₹500–600 daily, often less, and sometimes much more. Mama keeps the accounts carefully, saving and planning for the future, while Papa lives from day to day.

Their joint income pays for the rent of our house, my school fees and everyday expenses, but often there is no spare money for the hired rickshaw that takes my brother, Swastik, to school. The relationship between Mama and Papa is 'sweet and salty'— he teases her and she gently scolds him as if he is one of her students. Swastik and I are part of this teasing game, and our home is a happy one. In Marathi, Pune is called 'Shikshnache Maher Ghar', which means maternal home of education, and father says that our home is just that! We are a small family and live in Katraj, in two rented rooms on the ground floor, each of which is 10 ft x 20 ft. The men in our housing society work as electricians, office boys or have jobs in small companies, but very few women are allowed to work outside the home.

In our society, residents are friendly superficially, and there is a cold war situation. Recently, there was water shortage in the area. Our building was not affected, but had it been, no one would have helped those in need. People would have smiled and made up excuses to not share their water. My mom, brought up in a real slum, says people in slums are poorer but more helpful. Once, Papa's friend offered him the use of a nice rent-free home, but my father refused the offer, because he believes that we must live within our means and improve our lives through education.

Young men and women today are aware of the advantages of a good education and are willing to work part-time to pay for their schooling. But most parents from low-income families still feel that basic schooling is enough, and encourage their children to do full-time jobs from an early age. Neither the child nor the parent is right or wrong, it is just the difference between traditional and modern ways of thinking.

Between the ages of 10 and 13, when children are still close to their parents, they should be warned about the bad effects of drugs and alcohol. In our communities, both are widely used. Parents go out to earn a living, while the children, left alone, follow the not-so-good habits of the older kids around them. Younger children, always thinking they are more grown up than they actually are, experiment with liquor and drugs and by the time they realize the bad effects, it is too late.

The security of our small family was shaken on 24 May 2013, when my father had a serious accident. He was riding pillion on the bike of a friend, who, being drunk, lost control of his vehicle. Papa's knee bone was shattered into powder-like pieces and he was hospitalized for four months. My mother stayed in the hospital with him, and Swastik and I went to live with an aunt. When the teachers at my Akanksha KCTVN school heard that we did not have the money to pay for the hospital expenses that were mounting up, they contributed ₹26,000 from their monthly salaries. Their generosity had a huge emotional impact on me, and I promised myself that I must always try to help people in need. It also made me fiercely loyal to my school, for, by this act of giving, the school and teachers, became my family.

Fearing that my dear father would die, I was very distressed and Rupali Didi, my science teacher at KCTVN, helped me stay strong and calm, sharing with me her own emotional trauma when her father was ill. Didi is now abroad, but whenever I think of her, especially in times of need, tears roll down my cheeks. In the English composition class in Class 10, we had to write a letter of gratitude—I addressed mine to Rupali Didi. She read it, came up to me, gently put her hand on my shoulder, smiled, and said, 'Thank you.' I am not sure of all the meanings of the word, 'wow', but whenever I think of Rupali Didi, I say to myself—'wow!' She had a deep understanding of children and when Rohit, one of the students, misbehaved, instead of scolding him, she explained to the class, 'He has picked up this behaviour from his surroundings—we must all help him to do the right thing.'

I was 7 years old, in Class 3, when I passed the entrance examination for KCTVN, a school where education is based on these four pillars: excellence, perseverance, achievement and change. Every year, awards are given to students who have made a change in themselves, and one year, I was thrilled to receive an award from Rupali Didi. The school's philosophy encouraged us to compete, not with others, but with ourselves.

The teachers at KCTVN did not tolerate any form of discrimination or physical abuse. But since eve-teasing and bullying did occur, a Student Council was formed to deal with these issues. There was an incident where a girl at a bus stop was surrounded and humiliated by a gang of boys. One of these boys was in our school, and the Council acted quickly and suspended him. I became determined to protect girls from any form of abuse.

A school is a place of learning, and KCTVN was definitely that, but it was also a shelter where I was safe. Once, during the morning assembly, Shalini Didi told the students that we were all part of one family. I believed her, and immediately felt more comfortable. I was accepted the way I was—crazy, funny, sweet, popular, quiet and, I hope(!), a mature girl. Yes, I belonged in this school. Everyone emphasizes the importance of education, but at KCTVN we were showed, in a hundred different ways, not just the importance but also the results of education—the benefits to us and to those around us.

When I look back on my schooldays, there are only good memories. It was the teachers who made our school the amazing place it was. If we did not understand something, they used every method they knew to make us learn it—Web diagrams, videos and PowerPoint presentations. What we could not tell our parents, we shared with our didis and bhaiyas. The girl who was teased at the bus stop was frightened to tell her parents about the incident because they would stop her from attending school, but she had no fear of the teachers. KCTVN was not an ordinary school.

As I was growing up, India's social problems were all around me, but it was at school that I became sensitive to them. With Amar Pol, our teacher, I took the first step towards solving a small problem. On a field trip to a school for the blind, we cut the grass that had overgrown in the compound. The task was small, but when we had finished, the compound looked neater and was a nicer playing environment for the students. It was a good feeling to make things better for other people. My best friend, Kshitija, felt the same way, and, on 15 August 2015, with the encouragement of Shalini Didi, we founded We Are Change, an NGO that is committed to identifying and solving social problems.

Our first goal is to make changes in the education system. Unfortunately, many of the teachers in the PMC schools are totally disinterested in their students. They spend most of the day sitting outside the building and chatting. If the children misbehave, they are brought out in the hot sun, told to bend down, touch their toes and stay in that painful position! Another malpractice is giving volunteer students certificates of attendance even when they don't attend classes. Every Saturday, from 7 a.m. to 11 a.m., we hold classes in the PMC schools. Using laptops and videos, we apply the creative learning methods that we learnt at KCTVN to motivate the students to enjoy learning. We hope that our enthusiasm will spread to the teachers! After we observe improvements in the school, we will move on to another place and take up another issue.

I have had many dreams, wanting to be, at different times, a psychologist, an actress, a counsellor. My interest in these three careers grew out of my love for the movies. I am a total movie buff. The different characters in films, with their different traits and different responses to the same situation, fascinate me, and have sparked my interest in the way people think and react.

My favourite movie hero is the Marathi actor Swapnil Joshi. He is not only a great actor, but also a caring person and treats women with respect. Swapnil was once in a mall surrounded by fans (including me!), when he noticed that one of the girls in the crowd had injured her foot. He took her aside and helped her get out of the crowded area. Another story about him is that he flew from Mumbai to Delhi just to eat his favourite kind of kebab! I am pretty impulsive too and when Swapnil Joshi came for a promotional event to our college, I took a selfie with him. These are small, probably silly, incidents, but they sort of made me feel connected to him.

After Class 10, I looked at career options—science was too tough, arts and commerce were not for me and psychology did not work out. So, I opted for a diploma in Information Technology at Maharashtra Institute of Technology Polytechnic, Pune. In my first unit test, I scored 93 per cent and decided that this was the career stream I would pursue. After my diploma, I will do a degree in Engineering and qualify as a professional IT engineer.

Leaving KCTVN does not mean going away, for Akanksha's commitment to its students never ends. There is a strong bond among Akanksha's alumni and we have an active mentor programme. The alumni often meet in the Akanksha office and have stimulating discussions. I recall a very active conversation we once had on defining role models. We ended the discussion by listing, not the names, but the qualities we admired in different people—creating our own composite role models. It was like putting the best of different chocolates in a jar, to make the eating more worthwhile.

For all the good qualities they have, and the hard work they do, Mama and Papa deserve a comfortable life. They have provided my brother and me with whatever we needed, though sometimes, we had to wait for it. I have never felt any anger or envy towards the rich, but when we need money urgently, I wish we had more of it. For example, Papa has to have surgery on his leg; if we postpone the operation, his pain will increase in the future. In a while, we will be able to afford the operation, but at such times it would be nice to have lots of money. When there is a difficult situation like this, I stand in front of a mirror and tell myself, 'I can handle this problem,' and somehow I get the energy and confidence to deal with it. Inside me, I know that the values my parents have given us—not to cheat, to give 100 per cent of ourselves to whatever we do, to oppose the bad and encourage the good—are more important than the money we don't have.

My teachers have repeatedly said, 'Be positive. Be positive. Be positive.' And that is what I tried to do when Kshitija and I went to Bengaluru for the Ashoka Foundation presentation. To help us expand our NGO activities, we had applied to the Ashoka Foundation for funding and training support, and were invited to Bengaluru to present our work to the selection jury. Before the interview, I was very nervous, and began to talk to myself:

Question: Why nervous?
Answer: Afraid.
Question: Afraid of...?
Answer: Not getting selected.
Question: What will happen if I don't get selected?

Answer: I will return with the memorable experience of having presented my organization to a jury of important people!

Question: Then why am I afraid?

With confidence, I went before the jury. Kshitija and I rocked the interview, and came out as winners! We Are Change will now get training support for a whole year from the Ashoka Fellowship. What a proud coincidence for us that twenty-five years ago, Shaheen Didi, the founder of Akanksha, had also presented her Akanksha Centre model to the jury in Bengaluru, and was made an Ashoka Fellow. The Akanksha wheel that Shaheen Didi first turned is still spinning...and from it, Kshitija and I have spun off a new one.

∽

'When there is a difficult situation, I stand in front of a mirror and tell myself, "I can handle this problem," and somehow I get the energy and confidence to deal with it.'

PRIYANKA PARIT | AKANKSHA | 1994 TO 2010
BCom (Jai Hind College), MCom (Sydenham College), Mumbai
MBA student, Jamnalal Bajaj Management Institute, Mumbai
Senior Sales Executive, Magic Tours of India
Date of Birth: 7 July 1991

NEW WORLDS TO CONQUER

I was looking for something exciting to do after my Class 10 examinations. At the same time, Deepa Krishnan, a graduate from the Indian Institute of Management, was recruiting part-time tour guides for her travel company, Mumbai Magic Tours. The Akanksha organization introduced me to Deepa. It was a perfect match. My first job was taking foreigners on offbeat tours of Mumbai. With them, I discovered parts of the city that I never knew existed and earned ₹700–1,500 for each day that I worked. Those were the best days of my life.

I was introduced to Akanksha when I was 3 years old, a long time before I met Deepa. The first Akanksha Centre was located in the Holy Name High School in Colaba, and every afternoon, a green bus would pick us up from our homes in Ambedkar Nagar. It was a fifteen-minute ride to the school and I always got to the bus stop really early, to be the first in the queue and get a window seat!

Six months later, I was enrolled into the Holy Name High School as a full-time student—one of the few community children to get admission in a government-aided private English school. Memories of school float around in my mind. There were sixty-five children in one class and the teachers never remembered our names. I was shy and scared, and after being beaten regularly on my knuckles, I stopped participating in class. Sports challenged me—I excelled in running, did well in the heats, but in the finals on Sports Day, I got nervous and, never won any medals! The school was good, but I just did not work hard enough and my scores fluctuated—I struggled until Class 7, was among the top ten students from Class 8 to Class 9, slid down in Class 10 and finally zoomed up and got a distinction in junior college!

One moment stands out in an otherwise average school career. I was recommended to be the Head Girl and had to give a speech during the school assembly. I lost the election, but the pride I felt speaking in front of the whole school gave me confidence. And all the teachers suddenly remembered my name!

After school ended at 3 p.m., the empty classrooms on the ground and first floors were converted into the Akanksha Centre. In my regular school, I was hesitant to put up my hand even if I knew an answer; at the Centre, I was the first one to jump up with the correct answer. In school, I was not popular, but at Akanksha, everyone knew my name.

Our experiences at the Centre were varied. On class trips, we visited villages and met children whose condition was much worse than ours; we learnt to modulate our voices and sing in musicals; and were comfortable when we were taken for projects to a five-star hotel. Every day, I waited for school to end—and the Centre classes to begin!

The Learning to Lead (LTL) Programme at Akanksha had the biggest impact on me. There were just ten students in the group, and in the five years that we spent together, we developed strong bonds that remain even today.

I was 13 years old when I did my first research project. The subject was public distribution—a topic that was part of our daily life. Amma would stand for hours in long queues to buy kerosene, and was given only one or two litres, instead of the official allotment that was much more. This made me very angry. During the project, I boldly went up to the man in charge, and questioned the distribution system. He patiently listened to me and explained that the demand was greater than his supply. But the truth was very different. There was a shortage of kerosene supply because the distributors were selling the stuff in the black market! Once bottled gas was available, we did not use kerosene and the crooked distributors could no longer cheat us! I added all these points to my project, along with some statistics from the Internet. It was good training for college work and convinced me that I could improve the situation around me.

Priya Didi and Purvi Didi, my LTL teachers, are like my family, and I share everything with them. Priya Didi understands me even more than my own mother. She taught me that working on tight schedules can make the impossible, possible. She also forced me to think more deeply before answering a question, asking me again and again, 'And then what...? And then...?' Thanks to her, I have become more determined and focused. I know if I ever need help, even at 3.30 a.m., she would be there for me.

Purvi Didi is a true friend. She was my teacher for ten years, and I cannot forget the things that she did for us. During the tense days of the Class 10 boards, she came to the exam centre every day, waited for three hours until we finished and then took us back home. Our parents never did anything like this for us. It is this caring that made a difference to my life and taught me values that I could never have learnt in books. Priya Didi and Purvi Didi will stay forever in my heart.

My parents were the first in our community to send their children to a good school, and later, others followed their example. Both my younger siblings (I love them when they don't bully me!) were also in an Akanksha Centre. In 2016, my sister, Renuka, graduated in Humanities from Sophia College, Mumbai. She works with the client service team of Magic Tours of India, and is saving money for a fashion styling course that will cost around ₹2.5 lakh. Her short-term goal is to purchase a brand new car! My brother, Vinod, is the youngest and the most spoilt one in the family. He studies Commerce at Siddharth College, and assists Papa in his contracting projects.

Having secured a distinction in Class 12 in Elphinstone College, I transferred to Jai Hind College, another prestigious institution, and graduated with distinction in BCom. Keen to get into the hospitality business, I applied to the Dadar Catering College, and cleared the admission test. But the course fee was ₹3.5 lakh, and adding the extra expenses for field trips it was an impossible figure for me to put together. So I chucked catering out of my mind, shifted my focus to Commerce, and succeeded in getting an MCom degree from Sydenham College, one of the city's top Commerce institutions. I am now in the MBA programme at Jamnalal Bajaj Management Institute (attending evening classes on weekdays, and afternoon classes on Saturdays and Sundays), and, of course, working full-time.

Amma and Papa never thought that their children would finish school and go to college. Both were construction workers and they met and fell in love at the Simla House building project in South Mumbai. They practised the same religion, but my father's parents strongly objected to the marriage because my mother's family came from a lower caste. Even today, we are not welcome in Papa's village, and I have never seen my father's parents. Papa, a quick learner, picked up carpentry and masonry skills on the site and is now an independent contractor. He never went to school, but can read and write a little in Hindi, and uses WhatsApp to send price rates to his customers! I am so proud of him.

Every day, after cooking our breakfast and dinner, heating the water for our baths and packing our 'dabbas' (lunch boxes), Amma used to leave the house by 8 a.m. to work as a cleaner in several homes. She worked seven days a week and never got a holiday. It is easy to communicate with her for she is my closest friend. She helps me look at problems with a different perspective; when I judge situations or people too quickly or harshly, she makes me think positively. Sometimes, I am too dependent on her, and the maturity I think I have disappears whenever she is with me!

Although my parents are uneducated, they have an instinctive understanding of the important things in life—values matter more than material things. We never had too much money, yet it is surprising that the lack of it was never an issue, because we never wanted anything fancy. Every Diwali and Christmas, each sibling got a new pair of clothes, the rest of the year, my sister and I happily shared our outfits. Clothes have never interested me. It was only in college that what one wore seemed to matter and I felt a bit left out.

Papa and Amma gave their son and daughters equal education and attention, in fact, Papa favoured his girls! My parents' attitude towards money was also quite exceptional. Papa always insisted, even in times of financial need, that I spend all my earnings on myself. So from the age of 16, I paid for my tuition and college fees. I only bought what I could afford. Once I had saved enough, I made a list of what was required for college—a pair of jeans, T-shirts, sandals, handbag and so on. Then I ticked off the items I could afford to buy and went shopping!

We live in Ambedkar Nagar, in South Mumbai, a mixed community of Hindus, Muslims and Catholics. The houses are tightly packed between the high-rise luxury apartments of Cuffe Parade and the Arabian Sea. Even a slum has different income levels. The poorer homes are next to the mangrove swamps, the better built houses stand near the main Cuffe Parade Road. We had a 10 x 10 ft room where the five of us slept, and we rented out the upper storey. When I was 18 and earning really well, I renovated the rooms, and made them more pukka. We have now built a terrace, redone the toilet and kitchen and can afford to occupy both upper and lower floors. The kitchen is downstairs, with a space for my parents to sleep. My sister and I share the upper level and my brother loves sleeping alone on the terrace. Two big cupboards are plenty for our clothes! Amma does not need to earn now, but she gets bored sitting at home, and goes out to work for just two hours a day.

There used to be only tin and plastic shacks in Ambedkar Nagar with no water, electricity or sanitation. Now, it has uplifted itself with pukka houses, indoor toilets and running water. The latest and most welcome change is the daily sweeping of the narrow gullies by the municipal workers. We live here among people who are generous and sharing. Upon returning from holidays in their native places, friends bring gifts—rasgullas from Kolkata or jackfruit from Kerala. Our neighbours have become our extended family; and if we need any help, they are the first ones to arrive.

I have bought a flat in Vasai to give my family an opportunity to move out of the community, but Amma does not want to leave her friends. I will rent it out until we decide to move in, for at present, I can't think of living on my own. But just owning my own apartment makes me feel secure and independent.

My working career, which began when I was a part-time tour guide at 16, went on to become a full-time job in college. Today, as a senior sales executive in Magic Tours of India, I manage many things, from accounts to operations—assigning guides, researching suitability of tourism in different cities, planning and pricing tours and so on. It is a small firm and if someone is on leave, the job is handled by another colleague, so that there are no delays in getting the work done. Regardless of designation, caste or religion, every member of the team is treated with respect and my job is to manage without putting down anyone.

There is still a lot to learn. I make high demands on myself and sometimes being too rigid and impatient, I am unreasonable in my expectations of others. It is also not easy for me to accept different points of view. Parveen, my childhood friend, an Akanksha alumni, works in the same office and calms me down whenever I am stressed out.

The heart of Magic Tours is Deepa—my boss and mentor for eight years. She works from home and trusts me completely to run the office and handle the daily large cash transactions. She is also very understanding of any mistakes, even if it involves money. Each mistake, she says, is a lesson to be learnt. The transparency with which the office is run, makes it a healthy work environment for all employees.

Apart from enjoying what I do, I have a deep emotional attachment to Deepa and the company. It is her understanding and flexibility that made it possible for me to study and work simultaneously for so many years. My days are long with postgraduate studies and a full-time job that doesn't end in the office! To balance my life, I go jogging at least twice a week. It is my time, without a phone or laptop—a great way to work off the tension!

In 2014, I took my parents to Rajasthan, Shimla and Manali. It was the first time they had ever left Mumbai and seeing them so happy, I got the biggest thrill of my life. Of course, my father, as always, insisted that I should not spend too much, and paid half of the travel expenses!

It is fun to think ahead. Exploring India tops my list—Varanasi, Gulmarg, Puducherry, Siachen, Lakshadweep islands—trips that will give me first-hand information to pass on to clients and building up the reputation of our travel company. Also on the list is backpacking across Europe, cycling in Turkey and Budapest and walking through the English countryside. My passport is ready—I just have to wait for the right time to set off. Sometimes, I dream of how my life would have worked out if I had been born in London, with the whole of Europe so close to visit. But then I wake up, grateful for where I am, and what I have. There are no definite career goals at present; I will wait to see what turns my life will take...

At an Ashoka Fellowship meeting in 2015, I met young men and women dedicated to doing social work, and it made me rethink my own ambitions. 'Had I got my priorities wrong? Was I just chasing money? What about social responsibility?' But I hope that when the time is right, together with my LTL gang, I will start an after-school project for low-income students who drop out of school or are on the street after school ends. The Akanksha model was a perfect solution for me and it is now my turn to empower kids.

I never regret the place that I was born in, because it was my poor circumstances that led me to Akanksha's incredible teachers and mentors. The students in my college are better off than me, but I am more privileged because I have had experiences that they may never have. My children, when I have them, will have even greater opportunities and a better standard of living.

Most of my friends are married and when my parents discuss my marriage, they get tensed, reminding me, 'Sab achchay ladkey chale gaye' (all the good boys are gone). I don't want an arranged marriage, but looking around, the choices are limited. The community boys 'are way behind'! I want a husband with whom I can have an intelligent conversation, someone who earns more than me, and is at least a graduate. Also, I have no time to meet suitable boys! My working hours are from 9 a.m. to 9 p.m. and I am so exhausted on Sundays that I sleep most of the day! But when I look into the mirror, I like what I see—I am young, I am ambitious, I work hard and have a loving family. The rest will fall into place.

∽

'I never regret the place that I was born in, because it was my poor circumstances that led me to Akanksha's incredible teachers and mentors. The students in my college are better off than me, but I am more privileged, because I have had experiences that they may never have.'

AMIT DEOKAR | AKANKSHA | 2007 TO 2013

BSc first year, Azim Premji University, Bengaluru

Date of Birth: 24 November 1996

IN AWE OF SCIENCE

I was introduced to science in Class 6 and immediately fell in love with the subject. The topic was 'buoyancy', and Sangeeta Didi gave us an example of a woman who went to fetch water from a well. The minute the bucket was lowered into the water, it became buoyant and weightless. How did that happen? What were these strange forces that acted on and around us? Science fascinated me.

Through the Wormhole, a science programme on the Discovery channel, unfolded a completely new world to me—cosmology, quantum science and physics. In the episodes, Morgan Freeman asks larger-than-life questions, and the answers have competing theories. Every night, before sleeping, I observed the sky and admired its beauty. The universe opened up before me and I made an important discovery—science has answers to practically every question I ask; mathematics is a gift so consistent and true, no matter where we are in the universe. I stood in awe before science. How lucky I was to enter its world!

Papa and Mummy never had a chance to think about these mind-bending discoveries; all their energies were exhausted in getting enough food to feed their family three times a day. We lived in the Yerwada neighbourhood of Pune—a giant and profitable sector with industry, business and IT offices. As a young boy, I used to walk past the corporate buildings and smart cars parked in front of them and imagined being part of that glamorous world. But it was a distant dream, for the reality was that we lived in Yerwada gaon—a village but not quite a village, a slum, but not as congested as a slum—just a poor area with such narrow lanes that two motorbikes could barely pass through at the same time.

Every couple of metres there were open drains, and before the houses were fitted with toilets, we used common public facilities that were 100 metres away from our home. Our family of five, which included my grandmother, got our piece of the shade in a very small house. It had two rooms and the outer room contained our kitchen, bathroom, parking space for my dad's cycle and a shoe rack. Seven small steps took us from this outer room into the inner space, which was about the same size. Here, four of us would sleep close to each other, on one mattress. My grandmother slept in the outer room. After Class 5, I shifted to my grandmother's house in the centre of the city, and lived with her until I finished school. When I was a child, I never noticed the low height of the ceilings in our rooms, but if I went there today, my head would surely touch the ceiling! We now live in a proper rented house.

Most of my childhood was spent in those two rooms, and memories—both good and bad—are still fresh in my mind. The worst ones are of my father, an alcoholic, who never gave Mummy enough money to feed us. Papa worked in the canteen of an insurance office, but he was always taking loans from moneylenders and could not pay them back. The situation must have become too difficult for my mother to bear, for one day we came home and found her in the inner room, hanging from the ceiling. Fortunately, we reached home just in time to save her. Neighbours made her understand that she must have hope and that things would get better. After that day, my mother became stronger, never panicked and worked hard to bring up my sister and me in the best way she could. Mummy is, without doubt, the bravest woman I have ever seen. After that incident, my father stopped his unhealthy habits, got on with his work, and in the end things worked out OK.

All the bad began turning into good the day I enrolled in KCTVN school. We had waited patiently in the queue to complete the admission formalities, and when I was accepted, Mummy was full of smiles. It was Shraddha Didi who first welcomed me to class. The chairs in classroom 5A were so new that the factory plastic covers were still on them! My chair was yellow and I felt as happy and bright as the sun. The first question I answered in class was asked by Madhavi Didi, 'Who is the President of India?' I raised my hand at once: 'A.P.J. Abdul Kalam.' Everyone clapped and Didi drew three stars on the back of my hand. I was thrilled by Didi's praise. I was 11 years old and had come to a very special place.

In my PMC primary school, the teachers completed their syllabus mechanically, and never worried about the kids' overall growth. Physical violence, abusive language and absentee teachers were all a part of my early education. For even the smallest misbehaviour, we were made to kneel down and hit on our hands with a long wooden stick. I expected the same in the new school, but it was very different.

Soon after I moved to KCTVN, the PMC school experiences faded from my mind, and I put all I had into my new environment. Kanchan Didi, who is simply an admirable person, read to us from *Harry Potter and the Sorcerer's Stone*. Working in groups, we recreated the Diagon Alley from the book, and built our own magical shops with the materials provided. The project made the book come alive and I began to understand that to be truly educated, I must explore the social, creative and intellectual ingredients within myself.

The KCTVN also made things better for my family. Mummy was employed as part of the cleaning staff. Her new job transformed her from a rough woman into a sensitive lady. She was always treated with respect, and was influenced by the open outlook and caring behaviour of the teachers. She continues to work at the school.

Being so passionate about science, it was certain that I would pursue a subject that is science-related. What other career could be as stimulating? My teachers guided me towards engineering—a solid, practical, science-based career. I kept that goal in mind and studied hard to qualify for a top engineering college. I did not make it. Did I not work hard enough? Or was my heart not in engineering? I knew I wanted a career in science, but I wanted something that excited me. My one regret is that school never advised me on the different options in the sciences. It was only later that Manoj Bhaiya, my English teacher, told me about the pure science course—Undergraduate Science Programme—offered at Azim Premji University (APU) in Bengaluru. The university has a great reputation, and when Bhaiya told me they were starting a BSc in physics and biology, I was really excited. I love physics and opted for that.

The formal procedure for admission at APU began with an introductory presentation by professors from the university. The application process was in three stages—an online application, a written test to check English and basic mathematics levels, and finally, a one-on-one interview with a panel of two professors. Of course we had to pass each step before we went on to the next. Finally, our written skills were reviewed and we had a last interview. If you cleared it all, you got through!

There is an interesting philosophy behind the admission process. The university was more interested in how well the student fitted into their programme; and how focused and curious he or she was to know more about the subject. Less important was the student's knowledge of the subject. I was also lucky because since this was the first time the college was offering the BSc degree, there were fewer applicants for the course and so less competition. When I received the news that I was admitted to APU, I was thrilled.

The university is in Bengaluru and I knew that being away from my parents and home for the first time was going to be difficult. On the other hand, I was looking forward to meeting new people, and exploring physics—my favourite subject. The social adjustment in college was easy. In a span of a few months, I became really close to the teaching staff and students, and we are now like a family. The student–teacher relationship at APU is as interactive as it was at KCTVN, and teachers take a great deal of interest in our personal, social and academic development. KCTVN gave me the freedom to explore with confidence, and at the university I am acquiring knowledge to explore much further. Shalini Didi says that I have become more mature and confident. I like to believe that too, but in my heart, I am still the same.

Studying at one of the finest universities in India, with state-of-the-art facilities, and returning home to simple conveniences is not an issue. I appreciate my parents even more. They have loved and supported me in whatever I wanted to do, respected my space and never said no to me for anything. Even if they had a financial problem, they managed their money so that my needs were met. My mistakes were pointed out to me, but always in a positive manner. When I told my parents that I wanted to be an engineer, they said, 'Okay, we will support you.' When I changed my decision to pursue a career in physics, they said, 'Okay, do what you want,' even though they knew that engineering would get me a higher salary. I have never felt any kind of pressure from them.

I am a student at the beginning of my achievement ladder, and certainly wouldn't call myself successful. However, I have learnt one thing—love what you do, and then let life just take you forward. It might land you into greatness, or it might not.

∽

'Science has answers to practically every question I ask; mathematics is a gift so consistent and true, no matter where we are in the universe. I stood in awe before science. How lucky I was to enter its world!'

VIJAY YADAV | AKANKSHA | 2002–2012
(WITH GAPS IN BETWEEN)
BA second year, Wilson College, Mumbai
Recovery Specialist, Altisource Business Solutions Private Limited
Date of Birth: 6 February 1995

AGAINST ALL ODDS

My ancestors came from the village of Sonwani in the Ghazipur district of Uttar Pradesh and led an awesome life. The family house had twenty-five rooms and a property that spread over 500 bighas (125 acres) of land. Father talked about the days when they owned horses, and made fresh fruit juice in deep wells with 50–60 gallons of sugar. Spoiled by this easy life, the men were too lazy to walk and rode on horses to the toilet situated outside! The family lived off the rich land, and whenever they needed money, a part of the property was sold off. No one thought about going to school.

My father was different. He had studied up to Class 10, but his mother-in-law (he was married off at a young age) made fun of his studies, refusing to give him candles to study at night—making it difficult for him to prepare for his final examination. Wanting to be independent, my father ran away from home and came to Mumbai. He never went back.

Mumbai was a good place for Papa to start a new life. He began by washing glasses at a lemon juice stall near St Xavier's College, and in a few years' time, had bought over the stall, and set up nineteen roadside food and drink stalls in different parts of the city. He was a generous man but the family complained that he sacrificed our needs to help the young men who worked for him. Every morning he went on his rounds—starting at the

St Xavier's College stall and ending his day outside the same college. My mother would tell us that there is no future in going back to where one begins. She pushed us to get an education—so we could keep moving forward.

I was in Class 6 when Papa died. It was not an ordinary death. His body was found hanging over a bridge, on a railway track between Mahim and Bandra—far away from the route he usually took from work to home. It was only after a week that we located him—in coma at the Sion Hospital. A few days later, he was no more. We still don't know how or why he died.

After Papa's death, my brother, Ajay, then 14, took over the responsibility for the family. But he was too young to manage father's business and Mummy was uneducated and had never worked outside the home. We had no choice except to go back to Sonwani in Ghazipur. Papa's relatives welcomed us, promising to look after my widowed mother, and send us children to school. But after some time, they said that we were a financial burden, and kept delaying our school admissions. We could not go to mother's village, for in our culture once a woman is married, her place is with her husband's family.

Ajay and I decided to run away to Mumbai. We went to Buxar, the nearest railway station, 60 kms from Sonwani. A bullock cart and a jeep gave us short rides and we walked the rest of the way. The journey to Mumbai took two days, and since we were travelling without tickets, we hid in the toilet every time the ticket collector walked through the compartments. As soon as we arrived in Mumbai, we telephoned Mummy to tell her that we were safe. My previous sports teacher at Akanksha (I am sorry that I can't remember his name) gave us ₹300 to restart our lives in the city. With that money, we put up a lemon juice stand outside St Xavier's College, in the same place that my father had set up his first stall.

Ajay was 14 and I was 12 years old. Business boomed. College students, office workers, football players from Azad Maidan—all stopped by for a glass of lemon juice. We charged ₹3 per glass and on a good day made ₹2,000 to ₹3,000. We ate well; and went regularly to see films. At night, we stored our water units, extra lemons and other equipment in an empty parking attendant's hut outside the college. It was a profitable three months, and then in just one night, everything changed!

We returned from the Navratri celebrations in our old neighbourhood at GTB Nagar, to find that municipal workers had emptied out the parking attendant's hut! Our juice-making machine and the money that we had hidden in the hut, it was all gone. The silver anklets that we had bought for Mummy were also stolen. With no money, clothes or juice machine, we were back to where we had started three months ago.

Mother advised us to stay with relatives in Malad until things got better. The Malad family—husband, wife and three daughters—lived in a 7 ft x 8 ft room with a TV and a refrigerator. There was absolutely no place for us. At night, we sat outside the room and got bitten by mosquitoes. At 4 a.m., when the mosquitoes magically disappeared, we would get about two hours of sleep—curled up in the autorickshaws parked along the pavement, until their drivers pushed us out as they began to go on their rounds. The food my aunt cooked was awful; the streets around us were congested. Hungry and unhappy, we began to steal garbage cans, cartons and tins that were stacked outside shops, and sold them for whatever money we could get.

Mummy returned to Mumbai and in compensation for my

father's stalls, the BMC gave us accommodation in Mankhurd. The living conditions in Mankhurd were worse than Malad—waste overflowed in the gutters, crime was widespread and ambulances with screaming sirens raced past. It was 2008. Water shortage and fights over water were common. Every day, I walked 2-3 kms to the water pipes, punctured a small hole in them and filled a fifteen litre plastic can to carry home. The whole process took three hours!

We chopped the mangrove bushes to light fires to cook on. My brother worked wherever he could—washing dishes, selling items, painting walls—and we lived on ₹600-1,000, his monthly earnings. We could have reopened my father's two food stalls or returned to Ghazipur, but my mother insisted that running roadside stands had no future, and to get the best education we must remain in Mumbai.

When things are bad, people say that they can only get better, but they can get much worse. We had gone to Ghazipur to attend a wedding and when we returned, our whole house was gone! The railways department bulldozed and demolished 950 homes that they claimed were built illegally on their land. Most people rebuilt their huts with plastic, bamboo, ropes—anything they could find. We shifted to the third floor of a half-built building on a construction site. The doors and windows of the apartments had not yet been put in, and we used the empty spaces around the building as our toilet. My brother was employed as a painter on the site, and every time he climbed up the bamboo machan (scaffolding) to paint walls that were six to seven storeys high, we watched—frightened that one day he would slip and fall.

When work at the construction site ended, Anjali Didi

I Dream Like You

at Akanksha organized for Ajay to be interviewed by Nokia. Ajay did not have any decent clothes to wear; he went for the interview in torn jeans, an old shirt and broken slippers! He had no qualifications and was definitely not well dressed. His chances were not good. 'Why should I give you this job?' asked the interviewer. Ajay boldly replied, 'I have a responsibility to provide for my mother and two younger brothers, and that is the strongest incentive to work well.' He got the job and we rented a small apartment in a proper building for ₹1,500 a month—a bedroom, hall, bathroom and kitchen all to ourselves.

Ajay was studying through the open school system along with a part-time job. He passed Class 10 and was transferred to the Nokia store at Ghatkopar. The new environment and new friends brought about a big change in his behaviour. He started spending a lot of money on himself, but I could not be too strict with him. Since the age of 14 he had supported a family of four—was it wrong that he now wanted to have a good time?

In between these ups and downs, Mummy made sure that we continued our studies. Ajay was already enrolled in an after-school class at Akanksha. My Akanksha admission interview was scheduled on the same day and time, as a malaria test I had to take at the hospital. I insisted that Akanksha was my priority and went first for the interview, passed it, and then went to the hospital. I was 5 years old, and I don't remember much about that interview, except that the teacher's name was Anjali Didi.

The Akanksha St Xavier's School Centre had two classes running together in one large room. Each group had thirty children, two teachers and two volunteers. It was a have-fun-as-you-learn kind of environment. Puzzles and games, questions and answers, counters and drawings—we learnt without knowing

84

we were learning. The Centre timings were from 2.30 p.m. to 4.30 p.m., but most days we stayed on until 7.30 p.m.

The teachers at Akanksha came from different communities and social classes. They were pretty and cool, and did not have moustaches like some of the teachers at my municipal school! The best teacher at the Centre was Anjali Didi. Her strictness never made us want to quit her class, and her love never pampered us. She taught me for ten years, and always had four plans to work with: if A did not work, she tried B, then C and finally D. Different plans worked for different kids; she made sure that every student was learning. I could not predict then, that she would become more than a teacher to me, more than a family member, more than a friend. She listened to my problems, shared her own experiences, encouraged me to study and paid for my college fees, uniforms and books. She never denied me any help.

Her three-fold mantra is carved into my brain:

1. The only key for you to succeed is education.
2. Always look at the bigger picture.
3. Set high goals for yourself.

For three years I had not been to the Centre, but when Ajay got a job and the family was settled, we both returned to Akanksha. I was sent to Mankhurd where the students studied at a lower level, but with the help of a few small lies, I got myself transferred to Anjali Didi's class! The first day was tough; I could not keep up with the other students. Making fun of me, the kids said I had only come for the vada pao and bananas that we got at the end of the class. To prove them wrong, I went home and worked all night—non-stop, studying on the difficult homework.

The next day, I was the first to raise my hand, and give the right answers! 'Wow!' said Anjali Didi. A year later, I was one of her best students.

Having also missed three years of attendance at the BMC school, I was put in Class 7 of a Hindi-medium private school. I was older than the other students, and not being able to write or read in Hindi, I was beaten regularly. The municipal school had a 'no-fail' system but I had to score a certain percentage to be promoted to the next class. I struggled on, but ahead of me was the big Class 10 board exam. Since all the other Akanksha students, except Sagar and me, had passed the exam, the St Xavier's Centre had shut down, and we were transferred to another centre. In this important year, we did not have Anjali Didi to teach us.

A year before the final exams, our financial situation had deteriorated further. Ajay's lavish lifestyle with his new friends left little money for us—the rent had not been paid for a year, the deposit money was gone and we had to vacate our home. Mummy decided to take my younger brother and me back to the village. I wanted to finish school but she protested, 'How will you study in Mumbai without food in your stomach?' She was right. But I was determined to pass Class 10 even if I had to sleep on the street and go hungry. When Anjali Didi heard that I wanted to continue studying, she offered to pay for my accommodation, food and studies.

I stayed with my Mama (mother's brother) in Malad and school was three hours away in Mankhurd! Classes started at 7 a.m. and I had to change three trains and walk a long way before I got there. Since it was impossible to do this every day, I stopped going to school. When Rakesh Bhaiya and Tushar Bhaiya, both social workers, heard about my problem, they found me a room in Kurla, only three train stations away from school. With a bag of clothes, a bed sheet and a towel that also rolled up into a pillow at night, I went to a room that was shared with four older men. A Maharashtrian 'aunty' cooked for us, but her food was so spicy that most days I could not eat anything. I left for school at six in the morning without breakfast, had no money for lunch, went straight to the Akanksha Centre and returned home at night—to an uneatable chilli-hot dinner!

My health got affected from lack of proper food, and being absent from school for three months, I was behind in class. I took the easiest way out and stopped going to school. Physically and mentally, I had given up—sleeping most of the day, conserving my energy so that I would not feel hungry, and staying out all evening to avoid the rough men in my room. Months passed. I sat for hours and cried, knowing I had let down my family and Didi.

There seemed only one way to end my problems in one go—suicide. I walked to a bridge above a railway track, ready to jump in front of an incoming train—when I suddenly realized that though my troubles would end, I would not be alive to enjoy the benefits of the problems being resolved! To give up this precious life because I might fail in an exam or disappoint people did not make any sense. I turned around, picked up my belongings from the rented room, and moved in with my friend, Sagar. Anjali Didi was furious when she heard that I had moved out of the rented room, 'Go back to the village,' she said, 'with your attitude, you have no hope of getting an education.' For the very first time, she had given up on me. I went to an empty playground, and for hours the tears just flowed... Sagar

I Dream Like You

and Amit (Manu) tried to comfort me, but I could not share my sadness with anyone.

The finals were in three months and in the preliminary test I had failed in all subjects except English. The school was shut for study leave in February, the exams began on March 3. I had twenty-nine days to study the entire syllabus; and had not attended school or tutorials for most of the year. I tried to be positive. I did not crib, I just studied harder than ever. My old mobile phone with a broken screen and no back panel, became my teacher. I recorded the answers to hundreds of previous exam questions on the phone and played them back twenty-four hours a day—walking on the road, sitting in the train or waiting for a bus. I took photographs of diagrams and memorized them. In the unused Mankhurd railway station, Ankit Shukla and I revised and re-revised maths and science topics.

It worked! I passed with 70.6 per cent! In English, I got 89 per cent—the highest score in Mankhurd, and my name and photograph were on the scholars' merit list. The teachers in my private school who had guaranteed that I would fail were speechless when they saw my name in the toppers' list.

I wanted to go to St Xavier's College, like the students who used to come to my father's stall, but my grades were not good enough. Wilson College, where I got admitted, was a different world—with well-dressed students from wealthy homes. Everyone spoke fluent English and for the first seven or eight months, I talked to no one and made no friends. After college hours, I worked at My Dentist, Asia's biggest chain of dental clinics. My salary was ₹6,000, and now that I could afford the college fees, I returned the Akanksha scholarship money. Finally, everything was falling into place.

Before my Class 12 finals, calamity hit us once again. Ajay was diagnosed with TB and was admitted to a hospital. Since most days and all nights were spent with him, I could only study while travelling on the train—college to hospital, hospital to college. I read my entire economics course in one night, and was completely exhausted when I arrived at the exam hall the next morning. Ajay had medical insurance (he was now with Sony) and we could afford to admit him to a private hospital at Ghatkopar. What a mistake that was! There was a conspiracy between the doctors who over-prescribed medicines, and the hospital chemist who took them back to resell. Patients were literally robbed!

The final bill was ₹54,000. After the insurance payment, and Sony's contribution, there was a balance of ₹30,000. Until we settled the bill, my brother could not leave the hospital, and every extra day he stayed, the bill amount went higher. I called Anjali Didi at 10 o'clock one night. 'Come right over,' she said, 'I will have the money ready for you.' The bill was paid and my brother left the hospital that same night.

The next morning, Ajay's condition worsened, he was vomiting and bleeding, his eyes rolled up and his tongue hung out. We ran from one hospital to another—in one municipal hospital, he was put in a room with criminals; the ICU in the Nerul Hospital was no better; in Sewri, the entire hospital building had crumbled down. By now, Ajay was paralyzed, and we rushed him to J.J. Hospital. I fed my brother through a nasal tube and sat up all night rubbing his feet as the doctor had advised. It was difficult to concentrate on my studies but I gave the exam, and passed with 72 per cent. At last, I was in first year BA, studying economics, psychology and history.

With Ajay's medical bills rising, I needed a higher-paying job. Jyoti, a friend from Akanksha, introduced me to Sitel India Pvt Ltd, an international call centre. I failed the first and second round of interviews. I could not understand the interviewers' questions or accents, but I needed this job and did some quick thinking—if I answered one of the easier questions in great detail, time would run out, and I would escape the more difficult ones. My strategy worked—I got the job!

Everyone at Sitel was formally dressed and well groomed—ironed trousers and shirts, polished shoes, well-cut short hairstyles. We had a nine-hour shift, and the office had a gym, cafeteria and even a bunker room for naps! I learnt fast, and soon understood the clients' different styles of speaking. The company offered overtime and I took the maximum—working sixteen to eighteen hours, bringing home a monthly salary of ₹25,000–30,000. The money bought medicines, food, paid our rent and my younger brother's school fees.

My mother never gave up on her commitment to educate her three sons. Amit, the youngest, is in Wilson College. After my second year of college, I took a break year as I had failed in some subjects and needed to reappear for them. I have now changed jobs and I am now a Recovery Specialist at Altisource Business Solutions—a call centre where the salary is good and the office is closer to my house. Ajay left Sony, where he was one of the toppers in sales, and now works for LG, nearer to home. His health is still not good and he does not take his medicines regularly. If he falls ill again, there will be another gap in my studies. However, all these issues do not stop me from planning my dairy farm—an ambitious project that is taking shape in my mind.

Harnaha, my mother's village in Bihar, is a poor but beautiful place, where the deer come out in the afternoon, and the cows graze lazily all day. The land is still affordable and a train station links it with nearby cities. It is in Harnaha that I want to set up my dairy farm. Agriculture, the main source of income, provides food but it is not a profitable occupation. Dairy farming is a good business. A healthy cow gives 30–40 litres of milk a day, 300 days a year, and if the selling price of milk is about ₹40 per litre, it adds up to a lot of money. My cows will be housed in clean sheds, and milked in hygienic conditions to produce healthy milk for families.

My goals are higher than just making money. In Harnaha I can make a difference to the lives of children, men and women. Parents there are unemployed, forcing children in bonded labour to spend their days taking the cows to the fields. My dairy will employ mothers and fathers, so that children are free to go to school. Ninety-nine per cent of young men of the village enlist in the armed forces because there are few jobs in the village. Employment in the dairy will give them an option of staying in their homes instead of migrating to the cities.

Women have even less opportunities in Harnaha. The educated ones only use their knowledge to read forms and write letters for the illiterate members of their family. The dairy will employ women to manage the finances of the business—a job that can probably earn them up to ₹20,000 a month. I could not change things for my mother but I can for other young women. Mummy says it will be shameful for her to go back to her village, but I want my farm to be in Harnaha.

My mother married at the age of 14, expecting to have a good life. But her in-laws taunted her and my father beat her.

I hated my father for this, but he grew up seeing his mother beaten, and did not know any better. I cannot forgive him but I cannot blame him completely either. The 'pati parmeshwar' (husband is God) concept is drilled into the heads of Indian girls and boys. They accept that marriage is a business deal, and, like commodities, brides are sold for as little as ₹5–6 lakh. This is total rubbish and things must change.

Learning never stops... Some day, I will go abroad, get a Master's degree and learn everything I can about dairy farming. I admire the energy of the older people abroad—they are active and interested in life, unlike in India, where even healthy 60-year-olds go to Hardwar and give up on living!

As I plan ahead, I think of Anjali Didi's words, 'Dream big, only then you will attempt to achieve your dream. Whether you do or don't is the second step, but it should never stop you in any way, from first dreaming big.'

୵ୌ

'In Harnaha, I can make a difference to the lives of children, men and women. Parents are unemployed there, forcing children into bonded labour to spend their days taking the cows to the fields. My dairy will employ mothers and fathers, so that children are free to go to school.'

Vijay's brother Ajay never recovered from his illness and passed away on 12 January 2017. He was 25 years old.

CHAND SAYYED | AKANKSHA | 2002 TO 2008
BCom, Poona College of Arts and Commerce
School Administrator, Savitribai Phule School, Pune
Date of Birth: 29 August 1992

FIVE LESSONS TO LEARN

Patil Estate in Shivaji Nagar, Pune, has about 1,200 houses standing so close to each other that in the rainy season you can step from one house door to the next, all the way down to the main road, without getting wet. Approximately 6,000 of us live in this maze of narrow lanes. Every afternoon, the women sit outside their homes with plastic basins, washing the family clothes, turning the lanes into streams of coloured water.

I was born in Patil Estate. My parents are from Burhanpur village in Madhya Pradesh. My father, Abba, who is a mason, came to Pune to earn a better living, and works at construction sites in the city. Abba studied only till Class 3, but is the most interesting person I know, and I never get bored when I am with him. He tells stories about his past, has a sense of humour and gives me lessons on life. Whenever I am with him, I learn something new.

Abba is also interested in music, and I sit for hours listening to him sing old songs and qawwalis. Ammi, my mother, is a housewife and has never been to school. We are a big family of six sisters and two brothers, and we all grew up in a 12 ft×12 ft room with a 6 ft high ceiling that we could easily touch if we stretched up our hands. Once I started working, we built an extra room, and now that four of my sisters are married, we have more living space.

Except for my eldest sister, all of us were sent to school. Four sisters and one brother dropped out for different reasons, and at different times. They were in the PMC schools, and they probably gave up studying because the teaching was not good. My parents tried hard to make my elder brother stay on, but he quit in Class 3 to work with Abba on the construction site—he still works there. My younger sister, an Akanksha alumnus, has passed Class 10, and will soon go to college.

The first Akanksha Centre in Pune was located near our community. Many parents were suspicious of this free after-school class and there were rumours that kids would be asked to do things against their religion, or even be forced to change their religion! Would the children be safe? Would they be taken away somewhere? My parents did not listen to these stories, and they were among the first ones to agree to send their children to the Centre. Very soon, others followed.

Trust built up quickly between our families and the teachers at Akanksha. At the end of each month, there was a meeting and parents saw for themselves what was taught in class. Whenever a child was absent, the didis did follow-ups—coming to our houses to check why the child was not in class. If a child was ill, a social worker immediately took him or her to a hospital.

From Class 1 to 10, I studied in Urdu-medium schools in Wakdewadi and Khadki Bazaar. Abba and Ammi were never called to discuss my academic progress and no one bothered to help slow learners. Teachers did whatever they had to do and not one thing extra! The other bad practices included beating, discrimination against certain students and insulting children during the assembly in front of the whole school. But the overall Muslim culture of the school was positive and traditional.

Teachers wore hijabs, and strict rules were followed on the mixing between boys and girls, as is expected in our culture.

There was an 'asmaan-zameen ka farak' (a difference as wide as the sky from the earth) between the PMC schools and the Akanksha Centre. The Centre was a place of beautiful culture and brilliant teachers. We were taught the way we wanted to learn. Children learn in different ways, and the teachers adapted their teaching to suit each student—there were tuitions for struggling kids, empowerment for the older students, career counselling from experts and exposure visits to social programmes and leadership talks. So much was put into those two hours at the Centre! Akanksha became my teacher, my mentor, my friend. Those days were memorable.

One of the projects we did at the Centre was based on the concept 'One vision, one world'. I remember it very well. Centres were formed into clusters, and a partner school or country was assigned to each cluster. For one year, we explored the history, geography, food and traditions of different countries, and on Republic Day 2008, during a two-day event, we showcased each country through drama, dance, handicrafts and a food court. It was called Sunshine Around the World; it was a ride to different places on a magic carpet! I was the narrator of the show and worked hard on learning my lines, even practising facial expressions in front of the mirror! In front of an audience for the first time, I was nervous, but with each word that I spoke, I grew more confident and at the end when everyone congratulated me, I knew I had done well. In the many special years I spent at Akanksha, Republic Day 2008 was extra special.

It was also my first lesson: *When someone gives you an opportunity, make another opportunity out of that opportunity.*

I was one of the seven students chosen for the Akanksha SLP. We were selected for our leadership, communication skills and for showing interest in social causes. The two years in SLP made me aware of the social problems around me, many of which were much worse than my own. It also introduced me to people who were change-makers and gave me new perspectives on social issues.

We don't think of waste pickers as change-makers, but they really are just that. Kagad Kach Patra Kashtakari Panchayat (KKPKP), a trade union of about 10,000 waste pickers and scrap buyers, was registered in Pune in 1993. The organization uses non-violent protest to protect the rights of waste pickers against exploitation by moneylenders who harass and control them. The union has established cooperative scrap stores where waste pickers get more money for their materials. At first, I really did not wanted to walk with the waste pickers who went from door to door collecting rubbish! But soon, I was humbled by the work they did, and started learning from them about the many types of scrap materials, and how each can be recycled. The one month I spent at the union opened my eyes to an important issue, and by the end of that period, I had developed the greatest respect for them. The internship made it clear to me that we must all work towards the disposal of garbage in our cities. I have become much more conscious about segregating different types of waste and try to influence others in my community to do the same.

The motto of SLP was my second lesson: *Be the change you want to see.*

Animals, too, entered the SLP training. Packs of stray dogs roam across Pune, and the ones who come to our area get beaten and become aggressive. I was scared of all dogs, and most other animals. An internship with Paws Pack, an organization for pet owners, changed my attitude. Paws Pack is a pet centre for people with busy lifestyles who need services for their pets. I interned here for a month and got exposure to the activities of an organization that gives top priority to the needs of animals. At the end of the internship, I understood that dogs, like humans, need a lot of affection and have their own moods. For the first time, I held dogs in my arms. My fear was gone!

In the second year of SLP, I taught English to the kids in Father Agnel's Ashram, which was 15 kms away from home. I carefully planned each session, for to give a good lesson, teachers have to be fully prepared before they enter a classroom. Playing games with the children, preparing worksheets and organizing sports activities, I earned the respect of my students; and when the project ended, it was difficult to say goodbye to the kids I had grown to love.

At the end of these internships, I learnt my third lesson: *There is great joy in 'giving back'.*

Most teenagers at the age of 17 or 18 are not sure about what they want to study and during this period they need guidance. After clearing Class 10 with a first class, I consulted teachers and friends, and selected the Poona College of Arts and Commerce. Scoring 66 per cent in Class 12, I was motivated to study further. It was less than a month for the college academic year to begin, but Abba could not afford the fees. At first, it seemed there was no option except to leave college and work with Abba at the construction site.

However, determined not to quit college, I worked for three weeks, made enough money to pay for the first-term fees, and then asked my professors to permit me to attend college part-time so that I could continue to work. The college refused my request, but when I explained that to stay in college I needed to earn, they agreed. I attended the morning lectures and went straight to work. As my expenses increased, I needed to put in more hours at work. I went back to my professors and convinced them to allow me to come to college for a full day just twice a week. I don't know why, but they also agreed to this unusual arrangement—they probably saw I was desperate to complete my studies. My biggest challenge now was to manage the long hours at the construction site and keep up with college work. I passed my BCom with 59 per cent—the only graduate in my family. The marks were not good, but not so bad—for I was an average student.

My parents are proud of my achievements and this gives me great satisfaction. I am looking forward to getting an MBA and my goal is to become the operations manager of a big company in the social sector, an interest that is directly connected to my experiences in SLP.

My determination to get a degree gave me my fourth lesson: *Don't give up. If you want something badly, you can get it.*

Our didis used to tell us, 'Struggle is a part of life, you are special, and you can do it.' I struggled, graduated and got a job. I did do it. I am now a school administrator in Savitribai Phule School, an English-medium school for low-income children. The school aims to make every child an educated, empowered citizen, capable of taking independent and informed decisions. I handle government relations, coordinate stakeholders, manage school data and support teachers and school leaders. My manager says I am an asset to the school, and this encourages me to work with greater commitment. My reward is seeing the kids in my school get the same chances that I got at the Akanksha Centre.

The responsibility of a workplace culture is highly dependent on the manager, and Rahul Gupta, my Manager, is an example of hard work and commitment. He became the principal when he was 22 years old, and at 27, heads a team of forty-six employees and 574 students. He is a strong decision-maker, motivates employees and is good at problem-solving. Rahul supports his team members, urging them to take on leadership roles.

From Rahul Gupta, came my fifth lesson: *A leader is someone who creates leaders.*

I always loved playing sports. As captain of the Akanksha football team, I played football regularly for no less than five years. Even while I had a busy schedule, I initiated a six-month free training programme for community kids. We started the training with five players, and in a month there were thirty-five boys on the field. There was a strong team spirit and my own leadership skills developed with this experience. Cricket is another passion. These days, I am the opening batsman for my team and my Sundays are totally booked for cricket.

Ammi and Abba could never have guessed what an important decision they took fourteen years ago, when they agreed to send me to the Akanksha Centre. Education has enabled me to plan and make better decisions; my family has come to value my opinions and they support me when I encourage my nieces and nephews to keep studying. I am still learning to ask the right questions, and, in time, I will find the right answers.

✑

'My parents are proud of my achievements and this gives me great satisfaction. I am looking forward to getting an MBA, and my goal is to become the operations manager of a big company that works in the social sector.'

SONALI PAWAR | AKANKSHA | 2002 TO 2012
Bachelors in Business Management–International Business, First Class MBA
Marathwada Mitra Mandal's College of Engineering, Pune University
Administrative Assistant, Teach For India, Pune
Date of Birth: 22 March 1993

A THIRST FOR KNOWLEDGE

The second year of junior college was a downward turning point for me. I was 16 years old, and coming to a coed college from an all-girls school, I felt as free as a bird. I was a bright student and my parents thought science would be the perfect stream to build my future. Finding science impossibly difficult, I soon lost interest in studies, hung out in bad company and got involved in excessive social networking and creating online accounts. In short, I was heading for trouble! When the Class 12 results were posted on the board, I was the only person in my group with a backlog (which means I failed!) in the two most important subjects—physics and maths.

My friends had wealthier backgrounds than mine and I tried hard to be a part of their social life, and did not see that unlike me, they had fun but also studied. All of them cleared the finals with good marks—I was angry, jealous and ashamed, but I knew that I alone was responsible for my failure.

My problems did not end here. Mai and Bapu (my mother and father) discovered that I was dating an unsuitable guy and filed a police complaint against him, stopped me from attending college, and for a week I was not allowed to step out of the house. Santosh Bhaiya, a social worker from the Akanksha Centre where I was a student, stepped in to save me! He talked to my parents about the peer pressure I faced in the modern college culture, making them understand my teenage problems. A strong trust had developed between Bhaiya and them (they trusted him more than they ever trusted me), and accepting his explanations, Mai and Bapu permitted me to go back to college. Without Bhaiya's support, I would have been married off to some boy in the community, and by the age of 20, would have been an uneducated mother of three children! Thankfully, this is now a part of my past.

Our family history begins with my grandfather, who made a living in Mumbai, carrying heavy loads on his back and dragging goods on a wooden handcart. Grandmother lived in Humgaon, named after the goddess Humjai—a village near the hill resort of Panchgani in the Western Ghats. She woke up early in the morning, finished her housework and went to the wholesale market in Panchgani to buy fruits at reasonable prices. She then walked several miles to sell them in nearby mountain villages. It was a struggle for my grandparents to give their family two meals a day, but they put their earnings together, and sent four children to school.

Both my parents were born and brought up in Satara district. They moved to Pune after their marriage because the earnings from agriculture were not sufficient to live on. Bapu is a BCom graduate from More Vidyalaya College, but even in those days it was difficult to get a job, and he set up a small bicycle repair shop about a kilometre away from our house. Under a tent that was tied firmly to a tree, he patched tyre punctures, refilled air and fixed dents and brakes. Bapu always wanted to start his own business and never believed in working for someone else. When my uncle, who was a construction labourer, worked his way up to become a contractor, my father and his brother went into the business with him.

The three brothers got married and we all lived together—my grandmother (who came to live with us after grandfather passed away), my aunt and her two sons, my two uncles and their families and our family of five. It was a joint family in the real sense of the word! My grandmother now lives with two grandsons, and my aunt has expired. But there are still seventeen of us in one house, and to add space, we have built an extra floor. We are one of the few economically well-settled families from our village, who live happily, supporting each other.

Life in a chawl (a building with a common toilet and veranda) in Pune, is very different from village life. Our chawl has no official name but since so many families with the surname Shinde live here, it is called Shinde Chawl. Walking home down a narrow lane that goes off the main road connecting Kothrud to Warje, I pass Sai Baba's temple and Balaji's supermarket, and go by the sand vendor and the welder who are next door to each other. The community has an Anganwadi, a school for low-income kids that also functions as a community centre, providing meals for children, the elderly and pregnant women. Lanes criss-cross all around our homes, and at night cars and trucks squeeze into every available parking spot. Some houses are owned, others rented to migrants who come to the city to look for work.

I have lived in Shinde Chawl for almost twenty-three years. When I was a child, there were open, overflowing drains in front of our homes, stinking so badly that I covered my nose every time I ran past them. The houses were tiny and made of tin, mosquitoes buzzed all over and stray dogs and naked kids played near the open garbage. But this situation has completely changed. The houses are larger and well-constructed, and we have in-built toilets and electricity.

An awareness of the importance of education, especially among girls, came to our community in 2002. Children went to study at the Akanksha Centre after their regular school ended, volunteers came home to try and solve family problems and there were special tutorial classes to help children with schoolwork. I enrolled in the Centre when I was in Class 4 and stayed there until I completed Class 12. When the Centre shifted from Karvenagar to Wakadewadi, we travelled by bus, 10-12 kms each way. Many of my female friends were not allowed to travel so far on their own, and they stopped coming to class. Unfortunately, my brother too had to stop attending because the Centre timings clashed with his other tuitions. Now my parents regret that their only male child lost this beautiful educational opportunity.

English was the buzzword at Akanksha and students graduated with a fluency in the language. We also had early access to information technology—every Sunday, in computer classes, we were taught Excel, PowerPoint and other programmes. When computers were introduced in Class 7 in my regular school, I was way ahead of my class. Later, at job interviews, I was able to complete the admission tests correctly and on time.

Social service was part of the curriculum in every Centre. For the first time, I got new perspectives on child labour, gender discrimination, child marriage and domestic violence and took an active part in the popular street plays to spread awareness of social problems. As part of Akanksha's SLP, we visited two social service projects where Gandhiji's spirit lives on. The first was the Seva Cafe in Ahmedabad. 'Atithi Devo Bhava' means

'The Guest is God'. It is an old Indian tradition to be hospitable to guests in our home. At the Seva Cafe, this generosity is also shown to strangers. Customers are treasured guests and offered a free meal. If they wish, they can pay forward for the next guest. The guest before me had paid for my lunch, and I paid for the guest who came after me. It is a line of endless giving. All profits of the Seva Cafe support social service projects.

The second amazing organization was the Environmental Sanitation Institute, an NGO unofficially called the Toilet Garden. Gandhiji had fought against the practice of manual removal of faeces by the lower castes. The Safai Vidyalaya and its 'offspring', the Toilet Garden, established in 1985, trains people, constructs toilets, develops low-cost sanitation technologies and organizes environmental sanitation campaigns across India and the world.

Jayesh Patel, who we lovingly call Jayesh Bhai, supervises the Toilet Garden. He is a rare person. One day you see him cutting children's dirty nails in a slum, and the next morning he gives a presentation to senior corporate executives in a five-star hotel. For Jayesh Bhai, both are service. His father, Ishwar Patel, built 200,000 toilets, and established 118 organizations, including the Environmental Sanitation Institute. He was called Mr Sanitation! His advice to his son was, 'Don't carry heavy loads to change the world. Do the work that is connected with your heart, and you'll become an instrument of nature.' And Jayesh Bhai is just that.

Jayesh Bhai sees right into the centre of our hearts, making them expand with a love that we didn't know we had. 'You don't have to find love,' says Jayesh Bhai, 'it is within you.' I began to look for this love inside me and in the people I met, and I felt very good. In India, so many things need to change. Where do we begin? Again, I hear Jayesh Bhai: 'There is beauty and power in the small. Focus on what you can do in this moment. Relationships are important—build relationships instead of projects.' At different points in my life, I have stopped to remember his words. I carried my Ahmedabad experiences with me to junior college and began my first social service project—tutoring community children in science, maths and English.

In spite of my terrible Class 12 results at Shamrao Kalmadi College, I got admission into the Marathwada Mitra Mandal's College of Commerce in Pune. I had learnt my lesson, and now studied seriously—three years later, I graduated with a first-class degree in Bachelors in Business Management-International Business, ranking third in my college.

A day before my first exam, there was an incident that could have ended my dreams of a career. Returning home from college, I noticed Manisha Tai, a neighbour, sitting outside her home with an extra sweet smile for me. The moment I entered, Mai, my mother, took me to the last of our three small rooms, and gave me a sari to wear. The house was all tidied up; Bapu stood at the entrance anxiously waiting for someone to arrive. I guessed very quickly what was happening—my parents had received a marriage proposal for me and I was being dressed up to meet the suitor and his family. I cried and begged my parents to let me complete my education, but the boy had already arrived!

Every girl has an image of the man who is meant only for her—my suitor was not what I imagined 'my prince' to be! There was nothing impressive about him. He was of medium height with a dull expression. He did not say much and was not interested in anything I said! I mentally made up a list of his bad points—he probably smoked, drank, lied about his job and had failed at school! Maybe I misjudged him, and like me, he too might have been pushed into this meeting. I just knew that neither he nor his parents were right for me. When I announced to everyone in the room that I would continue with my studies and have a career, his parents quickly rejected me. If the proposal had gone through, Sonali's story would not have been in this book!

Most boys in my community are not as well-educated as the girls. Many families own land in their villages and lease out parts of the property. Their sons live off this easy money. There is no incentive for them to study or work, and so they spend the time roaming around the streets, and getting into trouble. How can I trust such boys? Their mentality is also weird. Even in this modern age, they expect their educated wives to sit at home, cook, clean and never have an opinion on anything! And of course, the women must give birth to one child after another, until a boy is born—a toy for the in-laws to play with! I cannot accept this way of living. I will study and have a career—that is the life I want for myself.

Not happy with my decision to continue my studies, my parents gave me a list of reasons why they should not invest the ₹2-3 lakh needed for my MBA degree. 'Instead of simply wasting this money we can use it for your marriage. With a big dowry you will go to a good family and not be tortured. Your in-laws will never allow you to go out of the house alone. What then is the use of getting all these degrees?' asked Mai and Bapu.

I guess it is true that spending on a girl's education does not benefit her parents, because at the end of it all, their daughter goes to live in some other house! It is also true that parents are pressurized to give a high dowry—a system that should definitely be stopped! A girl's family often feels that they are of less value than the boy's parents, and their status in the society will be lowered if they don't get suitable proposals. I try to understand these points of view, but fail each time. My parents are thinking of my well-being and maybe it is true that boys in our society don't want 'overeducated' girls. So who will marry me in the end? All this talk was very annoying and when my opinions were ignored, I felt like leaving the house!

The biggest hurdle I have had to overcome was convincing my parents to let me study further. Finally, they agreed to pay the fees for the two-year MBA degree. In the second year of my bachelor's degree, there was an opening for an Administrative Assistant at the TFI office in Pune, and encouraged by Santosh Bhaiya (my saviour after Class 12), I interviewed for the job, got accepted, and joined TFI on 10 October 2013.

My work responsibilities included maintaining a volunteer database, placement of volunteers, organizing orientation programmes and keeping financial records. I had opportunities to attend conferences, workshops, training sessions and perfect my English skills, all of which will benefit my future professional life. The TFI Fellows teach in low-income schools, some of which are managed by Akanksha. So, I am connected to two of my favourite organizations: Akanksha and TFI.

Hundreds of people go in and out of the TFI office—fellows, volunteers, donors, sponsors, visiting lecturers and schoolchildren. They come from various backgrounds and have different personalities, but they share a common belief—'All children will one day attain an excellent education.' I believe in this vision. My TFI colleagues are very well qualified, and sometimes I pinch myself to be sure that I am a part of this organization. Friends are always complaining about their colleagues, bosses and managers. I have no complaints at all. Lucky me!

If Akanksha shaped my childhood, it was TFI that influenced my college years. With the support of these two organizations, I am pursuing an MBA at Marathwada Mitra Mandal's College of Engineering at Pune University. In my final year, I will go for either Human Resources (HR) or International Business as my major topic. After the degree, I would like to transfer from administration work to HR; if that is not possible at TFI, I will interview for an HR job with a multinational company. I was just a kid from a low-income home but my bhaiyas and colleagues at Akanksha and TFI believed that I would succeed. Most kids have not been as lucky. Sooner or later, together with a career, I will teach and mentor community children (especially girls), helping them find their place in the world, just as I found mine.

Many of my childhood friends dropped out of Akanksha and school, and are unemployed. They spend their days doing drugs, drinking, gambling, abusing—stuff that gives me goosebumps! My parents sleep well at night, knowing that they have given their children a much better life than most families in the community. Pradnya, my younger sister, is a medical student. When neighbours don't believe that she will become a doctor, I tell them, '*Tab aa jaana ilaaj karane, fees nahi lenge aapse*' (when she is qualified, come for treatment, she won't take fees from you). My brother, Pradhyumna, is studying Civil Engineering. Both are Akanksha alumni. Earlier, my mother used to stitch blouses to make extra money, but since I have started earning I don't allow her to work and she enjoys just being a housewife. With god's grace, my lovely Bapu, Krishna, now runs his own construction business.

There are still many issues in the chawl—living in rooms too close to each other leads to frustration, jealousy and fights; no one wants the other person to get ahead; there is domestic violence; and parents continue to have narrow, old-fashioned mindsets. When I walk in the community, I hear the women whispering, 'She is already 22 years old and still they have not got her married off.' I smile, look around, and feel so lucky that my parents had the courage and wisdom to be different from the others in the chawl.

I cannot be absolutely sure whether a boy called Prashant will become part of my future story, but I hope he does. We have known each other for four years and he supports my decision to study and have a career. Prashant is a well-settled guy, running Skyline Trip Pvt Ltd, a travel company. Perhaps, at some stage after I get business experience, I will work with him and run one of his branches or even become a partner in his firm. Foreign exchange transactions interest me and maybe I could set up facilities for foreign travellers.

My parents oppose our relationship because he is from a different caste. This is an important consideration for them. I face a conflict: Prashant and I plan to get married in a couple of years, and yet, we don't want to hurt our families. If Mai and Bapu choose and are OK with a boy, they feel I must be OK with him too! But the boy they choose for me will most probably be very conservative, and not permit me to study or work after marriage. I will not be trapped in a house. Should I waste all the effort I have put into getting an education? Should

I let it all go, just like that only? My answer, 'No, I won't!'

In my heart, I am confident that in time, my parents will agree to me marrying a boy of my choice, as they did to my continuing studies. Thank god, I now have the tools and confidence to think for myself. One day soon, I know my parents will understand that.

∽

'When I walk in the community, I hear the women whispering, "She is already 22 years old and still they have not got her married off." I smile, look around and feel so lucky that my parents had the courage and wisdom to be different from the others in the chawl.'

KANHAIYA PAL | AKANKSHA | 1998 TO 2011
BCom, Lala Lajpatrai College, Mumbai
Executive, NPS Product Operation and Regulatory Interface,
National Securities Depositary Limited
Date of Birth: 10 June 1992

IMPLEMENTING THE LAW

Papa always hoped that I would be a lawyer. For many years, he has championed the rights of people in our slum community who have been treated unfairly by government officials. As a lawyer, I could help him to solve some of these problems—concerns that are close to his heart. My interest in law is also motivated by my desire to bring accountability and transparency to government welfare schemes. His dream for me has become my career path.

A recent incident has made it clear that I need to be well-qualified before I can make a difference. In November 2015, several homes of Akanksha alumni in the slum community of Gautam Nagar, Mumbai, were demolished. The families had to spend one night in the open, without any shelter, and the next day they were relocated to Chembur—a new and unknown area for them. Akanksha's Social Impact Team contacted my father and me to ask for help, but not having enough knowledge or the power to fight the regulatory body, we could do nothing. This was very frustrating—wanting to help but being unable to do so. Slum rehabilitation is taking place all over Mumbai; homes are regularly demolished, but alternative accommodation is not given in a fair and transparent manner.

I remember a situation when a neighbour's house was demolished by the BMC officials, but there was no alternative accommodation for him in the transit camp. Homeless, the poor man ran from pillar to post, approaching government corporators and MLAs—no one even tried to resolve his problem. My father filed complaints to government agencies under the Right to Information (RTI) Act, and finally he was allotted transit accommodation. It was a big achievement for my father. He had made a difference in someone's life, and this inspired me to do the same.

Satark Nagrik Sangathan is an NGO that demands accountability from the government. Working together with Vinita Singh, a member of the NGO, Papa and I explain the RTI to community members and help them file their grievances. When I surf the Internet, I find many welfare schemes for slum communities: issuance of ration cards, the Rajiv Gandhi Arogya Yojna (a free medical service scheme) and the Slum Rehabilitation Authority (SRA) that should allot fair space and adequate structure. But it is difficult, often impossible, to meet the relevant higher authorities, and implementation is blocked by corrupt lower-level officials. But we keep trying...

Our family is from Uttar Pradesh, where Papa went to college. My grandfather was uneducated—a farmer—but he knew the importance of studies—unusual for his time. When Papa came to Mumbai in 1992, it was not easy to find a job, for thousands of immigrants from all over India had come to earn a living in the city of glamour and Bollywood films. Papa started out as a hawker selling fruits from a handcart. He was married in his village when he was 16 years old, and he did not want us to make the same mistake. 'You must achieve something on your own before you settle down,' he used to tell my brother, Vijay, my sister, Laxmi, and me. Mother is a housewife, and although she has not been to school, she made sure that we sat down to study every evening.

I am blessed with the father I have. He is a BA graduate and understands the value of a good education. He disciplined us but was never too strict or physically abusive, unlike many fathers in the community. Papa understood the bad effects of alcohol and drug abuse and did not do either of them. He dealt with all situations in a civilized way. So I had a good start in life compared to many of my friends, who have memories of hunger and violence. Yes, I feel very blessed with my father.

Papa was a weaver, he later became a supervisor in the weaving section of the Century Textile Mills. His salary was not impressive but it took care of our basic needs. During the Mumbai textile crisis in 2007–08, when most mills closed down, it would have been easier for Papa and Mummy to pack up and return to the village, but they stayed put in Mumbai so that we could continue with our studies. Luckily, Papa was one of the workers who filed a case against the mill owners, and a court order entitles him to a salary until he is 60 years of age.

Clever with his hands, Papa constructed our 10 ft x 12 ft room with leftover planks of wood, bricks, sheets of plastic and tin. In the monsoons, rainwater poured inside, and we spent hours drying it up with old towels. Most of the year water was scarce, and I remember the days when we woke up at 4 a.m. and walked a long distance to fetch water for cooking and bathing. In 2012, as part of a rehabilitation project, we were given accommodation in a 180 sq ft concrete room, with our own private toilet. This was a big plus because we no longer had to wait in long queues at a public toilet. In a few years they will move us again—into a building with living space of

269 sq ft. That will be luxury!

In the Mariamma Nagar community in Worli, where we live, corruption is everywhere, garbage is not collected for weeks, and it is rare for a person to find any kind of privacy. But in the past few years there have been positive changes, and many homes have taps and toilets. Concrete buildings are replacing slum shacks. The biggest difference is the changing educational profile. The Akanksha Foundation has made parents aware of the advantages of sending children to school and college—now, about 80 per cent of the children in Mariamma are enrolled in schools. I feel sorry for the dropouts, many of whom don't even have vocational skills, and can only get badly paid temporary jobs. Those who are unemployed get into illegal activities and envy their friends who have made it.

As in many other communities, in Mariamma, boys are given special status and girls are not treated with respect. This worries me. Why should just being born a boy give one the right to do whatever one likes? In our home, responsibilities like cooking and washing clothes are equally shared between sister and brothers. Recently, and quite willingly, I washed my sister's school uniform because she was busy studying, and if she is late coming home after a tutorial class, my brother or I make tea for her.

My parents are also open in their approach to religion and social customs. Both Papa and Mummy practise the Hindu religion but they don't impose their beliefs on us. I respect my parents' religious views, but don't follow any rituals; my religion is doing good deeds.

I was sent to a Hindi-medium BMC school. The teaching was not as good as in convent schools, and later, when Papa realized the importance of English, he enrolled my sister in the English-medium Rajasthani Mahila Mandal High School. My school was only till Class 7, but Purvi Didi and Priya Didi got me admitted to the private Hindi-medium Marwadi Vidyalaya, where the curriculum included arts and design, computer literacy and sports. It was a big improvement from my BMC school, and luckily Dev Bhaiya persuaded the school to waive the computer charges (which were more than the school fees) so I could also take the computer class.

But my real education had begun on 10 June 1988, when I was put in the Akanksha Worli 1 Centre. I was only 6 years old, and for twelve years my life was filled with amazing experiences—I performed in musicals before an audience of a thousand, learnt to speak English, had meetings with senior corporate managers, visited the National Defence Academy and the Symbiosis Management Institute in Pune and spent time at the Indian Institute of Management in Ahmedabad. The Akanksha Centre was my Harvard University. Fired with my visits to these impressive institutions, and stimulated by my discussions with their students, I was determined to get an MBA degree from a reputed college.

Through my school years, I was guided by the didis and bhaiyas at Akanksha. Rajshree Didi could motivate the laziest and most disinterested student. Her sensitivity to social inequality and passion for social service had a huge influence on me. She introduced me to SLP—a 'parliament' where we discussed and debated social and global issues. I got opportunities to meet people from different professions, including Indian Administrative Service (IAS) and Indian Revenue Service (IRS) officers. These interactions broadened my mind and built my confidence.

I met Jayesh Bhai at Manav Sadhna in Gandhiji's Sabarmati Ashram, Ahmedabad. Dressed in a khadi kurta-pyjama and wearing leather chappals, Jayesh Bhai has walked through hundreds of villages, developing cottage industries and garbage disposal-and-collection services. He encourages villages to create jobs so that young men don't leave their homes in search for employment in crowded cities. Both Rajshree Didi and Jayesh Bhai believed that personal development must come before social service; both gave me an understanding of social work and how our lives can be richer because of it.

Purvi Didi and Priya Didi at Akanksha formed strong bonds with my family. They showed their love for us in so many ways— in 2008, when my father lost his job at the mill, Purvi Didi tried everything to find him work; before my Class 10 exam, they appeared at my doorstep with expensive nuts and dry fruits, so that I would be well-nourished for the exam; when I was ill they took me to the best doctor they knew and made sure I got the correct treatment; and when I lost my original Class 10 mark sheet, they ran in the monsoon rains from one lawyer's office to another, until they got me a second one. Together with Rajshree Didi, they have become a part of my biological family! Since I left the Centre, I don't see them as often as I would like to, partly because I feel shy to call them, and partly because I know how busy they are and don't want to disturb them.

After passing the Class 10 board examinations with 76 per cent, I got financial assistance from Akanksha's Learning to Lead programme, and went to the Lala Lajpatrai College. I maintained good grades, participated in the National Service Scheme (NSS) and in blood donation drives, and had good relations with the professors and the principal of the college. In my third year of BCom, I was nominated for the Best Student of the Year award. As I went up on the stage to collect my first honour in front of an audience of over 500, I felt so proud—as if I had been presented the Padma Vibhushan, India's second highest civilian award!

In college, I took my studies seriously, didn't party, smoke or drink alcohol, and was disciplined in my habits. My academic achievements gave me confidence, but being very shy, I didn't share my personal life with too many people. I don't know if people thought I was a 'nerd', but I definitely behaved like one! And the 'nerd' graduated with a first-class degree! I had met my parents' expectations. My father was keen that I continue studying; however, I decided to look for a job.

Together with studying for a BCom, I was doing a Chartered Accountancy (CA) course. Papa had paid huge fees for the CA tutorials; when I failed the Common Proficiency Test, his money got wasted and I gave up on my ambition to be a chartered accountant. I could not let Papa spend any more money on my education.

Through college placement, I got a job at Tata Consultancy Services, but left after a few months because I had reconsidered my decision not to study any further, and now wanted to go back to college. At this time, Deepak, a cousin brother had newly arrived from the village and was in need of a job. To help him, Papa took a bank loan of ₹20 lakh on a guarantee of his ₹10 lakh Voluntary Retirement Fund, bought a truck to transport construction materials and employed Deepak as the driver. Unfortunately, after a few months, Deepak decided to return to the village, leaving Papa to face the losses. My brother, Vijay, took on the responsibility of the truck, but Papa, worried that his studies would suffer, shut down the business. A lot of the loan money had already been spent; I knew this was not the time to ask father to finance my studies.

I uploaded my résumé on various job portals and got several offers. Interested in learning banking skills, I chose Kotak Mahindra Bank. I worked in the Customer Contact Centre Direct Banking handling Retail Liabilities Products, and coordinated with the branch and relationship manager and the back-end team. In November 2015, I moved to National Securities Depositary Limited (NSDL), which designs and manages e-governance projects and aims to implement them in a user-friendly and transparent manner. I also work with the Central Record Keeping Agency (CRA) for subscribers of the National Pension Scheme (NPS) and other NPS intermediaries, checking compliance documentations under the Pension Fund Regulatory Development Authority (PFRD). Professionally, I feel comfortable, and am able to share and discuss issues confidently with peers and the management.

The NSDL, where I work, encourages employees to improve their prospects, and I hope they will support my studies in corporate law. On my priority list are KC Law College, the Government Law College in Mumbai and the New Law College. When I chose a career in law, earning money was an important consideration. Good corporate lawyers make good corporate fees and I would like to take home a heavy pay package. But a part of my earnings and all my knowledge will be used to help those living in low-income communities be aware of their rights and assist them to get justice.

Papa is trying to adapt to modern times. In 2015, my younger brother, who is in his final year of BCom, was, for the very first time, allowed to go to a New Year's Eve party, and I was permitted to stay overnight at a friend's wedding function. Of course, we both had to provide satisfactory answers to Papa's many questions: 'Where is the party?' 'What time would it end?' 'Which guests are invited?' 'Would transport be provided?' Different generations think differently, and at home my siblings and I accept this.

I also accept the transition that I make every day—from the winding crowded lanes of the Mariamma community to the spacious air-conditioned comfort of the NSDL office, with a well-equipped gym, lunch coupons, canteen and library. In time, I know I can alter my financial situation. We have already bought a washing machine and a refrigerator, and our everyday needs are met more easily.

Having cleared the common entrance test for Law, I know I can and will be a corporate lawyer; I will own a luxury car, visit different places in India with my parents, go on adventure treks and valley-crossing trips, buy my own house; and perhaps, when I am 30 years old, have an arranged marriage! There are many dreams waiting to become realities...but today is good too.

৵

'My interest in Law is motivated by my desire to bring accountability and transparency to government welfare schemes and make improvements in the system.'

SUPRIYA DANDNAIK | AKANKSHA | 2007 TO 2012

BA second year (sociology), St Mira's College, Pune

Date of Birth: 12 January 1997

ANIMALS HAVE RIGHTS

It was in Kanchan Didi's English class that my life took two leaps—in two new and different directions. The first followed a discussion on the brutal product-testing methods used on animals. As Didi spoke, I felt the pain of the animals that suffer in the experiments and although I was not a hardcore non-vegetarian, I quickly decided to go totally vegetarian. My teacher, Manoj Bhaiya, encouraged this interest, and gave me a magazine on PETA India, an organization that fights for animal rights. I decided to join them in their fight.

Harry Potter was responsible for my second leap. After reading the Potter series, we did a project and recreated the world of Harry Potter, making the story come alive: we set up shops selling pointed wizard hats, long robes and secret drinks. Excited by the suspense and creativity in J.K. Rowling's books, and seeing the power a writer has to create new worlds, I wrote my first book, *Eight Nights of Learning*—a twenty-page booklet about animal rights. Since then, I have written more books on the subject, and plan to expand some of them, to publish at a later date.

Today, school is over and I am 20 years old. I grew up like most young girls around me, with my share of success and failure, happiness and a pinch of sadness. It took a long time for me to realize that sadness is like salt—it gives taste to the dish of life. Those who have never had to struggle don't experience the joy one feels when the hardship is overcome. The low points in my life were crucial to my growing up.

There are low points in Ganesh Peth, which I would describe as a backward area of Pune. I was born here in 1997, and my family still lives in the same place. There is no doubt that many places in India are backward, but the backwardness of my area is a matter of great concern to me. The houses are crowded together, garbage piled in corners and broken wires and metal scrap are everywhere. We now have a twenty-four-hour water supply, but people undervalue this facility, leaving the taps running and buckets overflowing! Alcoholism is one of the biggest problems. Many men are too drunk to work. Some die early from overdrinking, leaving behind young widows who are often rejected by their in-laws and left to bring up children on their own. The women in Ganesh Peth spend a lot of time gossiping, and their best pastime is to watch the saas-bahu (mother-in law versus daughter-in-law) serials on TV!

Superstitious rituals are blindly followed in our community. The Uttara Chowk is a small area where people go to frighten off the evil spirits. I really don't know whether to laugh or cry when I see them put sliced nimboos (limes) and green chillis marked with kumkum (a red powder) to keep away evil powers. What would happen, I ask, if the price of nimboos goes up so much that no one can afford them? Would the bad spirits be all over us? Then there are people who are too frightened to take long trips during the inauspicious amavasya (the no-moon days). Black magic is also practised on those who fall ill or have met with an accident. I am sure the cures would be faster and better if sick people were taken to a doctor instead of Uttara Chowk!

Mummy and Papa are religious, but do not have blind faith in anything. Sometimes, they wear the 'evil eye' to keep away bad luck, but they have never believed in black magic. I, too, have no time for ghosts or spirits; I believe in a God who is there whenever I need Him. And I am thankful that he sent me to live in Ganesh Peth.

I love the 'wada' we live in. It is an old building with many separate rooms, connected by a long veranda, and having common toilets, taps and washrooms. Pune's wadas and Mumbai's chawls are real examples of secular living in India. Just by chance, all, except two families, who live in our wada happen to be Hindus, but in general, different communities live together in harmony—celebrating each other's festivals, and visiting each other at any time of the night or day. On Diwali, rangolis are drawn in front of every doorway and delicious chaklees, chivdas (spicy snacks) and laddoos (sweetmeats) are made in different kitchens and enjoyed by all. Marriages are also shared occasions, where everyone participates in the ceremonies. When parents have to go to their village for an emergency, there is always someone to look after their children. Life must be different in apartment buildings—children do have the latest mobiles and computers, but I think they grow up in lonely societies, where people start and end the day without greeting their neighbours.

As years pass, wadas, like people, become old, and my sweet home is crumbling and about to collapse! Soon we will have to shift out, but I would have been happy to live here my entire life. Many residents don't feel this way and some have left Ganesh Peth saying, 'We want to move out of this dirt for our own good and our children's progress.' Papa and Mummy are happy with our home. The five of us share one room. We do have to adjust with the limited space, but it is still the best place for me. I have never wished to move into a big flat or bungalow. Any place, with people I love around me, is my home.

My grandfather was my first guru. He loved me like anything and taught me to read and write Marathi and good manners. Whenever I was with him, I felt nearer to God. My father, Tanaji Dandnaik, is from Palaswadi, a small backward village in Osmanabad. He is not educated, but is very intelligent and works as a rickshaw driver. Mummy has also not completed her studies but has done many different kinds of jobs, including screen painting, making agarbattis (incense sticks) and working in Annapurna, an NGO that provides loans to women.

Even when they faced difficulties, Papa and Mummy encouraged us to study. Shubham, my younger brother (who tries to dominate everyone!), has passed his Class 12 board exams and now aspires to be a mechanical engineer. My sister, Rutuja, who has finished school, has no definite career plans, but she loves Western dancing. Our parents never demanded a top rank from any of us, and maybe that is why we felt no stress when we studied and scored well.

I started kindergarten at the Jawaharlal English Medium Private School, but two years later I was pulled out because Papa's first workplace shut down and he lost his job. My younger brother was just born, and with another mouth to feed, and not enough money, Papa could not afford the school fees. My older brother and I were sent to S.G. Barve, a PMC English-medium school, where the fees were minimum, but there were no playgrounds or good washrooms. Sofia Gaikwad Ma'am, the principal, was a very good teacher, and taught us all the subjects. I topped my class and was considered a brilliant student—not a big achievement, since we were only three students in Class 1! Still, I felt proud to see my name pasted on a board outside the classroom. For students who were not academically strong, it was not a good system—their names never came up on the board.

If we had been living in a higher-income community, my brother and I would not have had the opportunity to appear for the Class 2 entrance exam at the KCTVN, an English-medium school for children from low-income homes. It was managed and run by the Akanksha Foundation, had a reputation for innovative teaching and admissions were very competitive. After I was admitted to KCTVN, my life underwent the biggest shift.

The teachers at KCTVN inspired every student to reach their potential and there was no division between the dull and intelligent students—both were given equal attention. I never needed private tuitions because my teachers were always ready to help me. The school was not fancy, it did not have large grounds, well-equipped libraries, laboratories or American-style washrooms, but it had what I needed—smiles, love, good teaching and encouragement.

We called our teachers didis and bhaiyas, and with them we shared our thoughts and talked about everything. Shampa Didi taught science so fabulously that I got good marks without opening a textbook. Monisha Didi introduced me to *The Wizard of Oz* and *Charlotte's Web*. History and geography became interesting subjects with Madhavi Didi, and Dhiren Bhaiya, who was tall and a little scary to look at, improved my maths. Prashant Sir was the calm and kind-hearted Hindi and Marathi teacher, and from Shalini Didi I learnt to be independent and fearless. After the bomb blasts in Mumbai on 26 November 2011, most schools in Pune were shut down. The KCTVN did things differently. We went to school as usual and learnt a lesson from Shalini Didi—difficult situations must be faced with courage, not fear. I have never forgotten that.

One of the experiences that will always stay with me happened during our school's annual day when I received a certificate for 'Research and Enquiry', from Anu Aga Ma'am. I remember how graciously she spoke to me, and when she saw me standing outside the gate, both she and her daughter waved goodbye. Much later, I learnt that Anu Ma'am was the chairperson of Thermax, a large corporation, and now she is a Rajya Sabha member. But, to me, she is a kind and caring lady who made a little girl feel extra special.

Every year, a few teachers left school—TFI Fellows who taught for two years and graduated from the programme or those who went away for personal reasons. I cried the day my favourite Sangeeta Didi had to leave. These farewells were sad but they brought us into contact with new teachers and new ideas. And then finally, school life came to an end—after a goodbye party that was awesome, we all went our different ways.

I was one of the first alumni to graduate from an Akanksha school in Pune, and I wanted to do a BA degree. But, I did not study enough for the school finals (thinking that Arts did not require high marks), and ended up with only 68.55 per cent. Papa, a practical man, said Commerce had better earning prospects than Arts. But when Kalyani Didi, the school counsellor, explained to Papa that the decision should be mine, he agreed, and I got admission to St Mira's College—the college of my dreams. I am now in my second year BA and will major in sociology—a subject that can help me discover my inner strengths. After that, I hope to do my Master's, and perhaps, go on to get a PhD.

The aim of my life is to work for animal rights, but to make a living I must choose another career. Animals and their needs are close to my heart and I will find a way to combine my career with my passion. Presently, I volunteer with an organization that provides shelter to wounded dogs until they are adopted.

One day, I hope our society will be completely free of animal cruelty. To make this happen, animals must not be used in circuses and other shows for entertainment. In spite of more people turning vegetarian, animal slaughter is a big concern and animal parts are commonly used for fur, leather clothes and accessories. Emulsifiers for cosmetics, soaps and detergents are tested on animals, and unfortunately because products that are cruelty-free cost more, people don't buy them. There is a lot we have to do to protect the rights of all animals, and, for different reasons, we are all guilty, including me. For though I love animals I am not always careful in what I choose to use, and there are times when I could have helped an animal but for some reason, did not.

I cannot pretend that I stand anywhere near those who go far out of their comfort zone to work for the welfare of animals. But I try to spread awareness on how we can be kinder and less cruel, and I will keep trying.

∾

'It took a long time for me to realize that sadness is like salt—
it gives taste to the dish of life. Those who have never had to
struggle don't experience the joy one feels when the hardship is
overcome. The low points in my life were
crucial to my growing up.'

PRASHANT DODKE | AKANKSHA | 1994 TO 2004
Class 12 (National Institute of Open Schooling)
Social Worker and School Coordinator, D.N. Nagar Mumbai Public School
Date of Birth: 30 November 1985

GIVING BACK

I had the best time of my life every time I got on a stage. I felt positive, confident and full of energy. Drama was my favourite class and I took an active part in every Akanksha musical. Each play focused on a special subject—communal harmony, friendship, leadership, etc. and that topic became a part of our curriculum, right through the year. In the musical, *Once Upon a Time in Shantipur,* I was Jaggu, the narrator and lead actor, and discovered that I could dance too!

Offstage, I helped with the soundtrack of the play *Operation Khazana,* and in two other musicals. I was assistant to Krutika Desai, a well-known TV actress and director. Krutika Didi was extremely strict, but I learnt a lot from her and just lived for the rehearsals and performances. I seriously thought about making theatre a career, but the reality was that I needed a profession with an income that would give my family financial security. But whenever an opportunity comes my way, I will jump right back on to the stage!

In 1994, The Akanksha Foundation had just been launched in Mumbai, and Shaheen Didi and Rumana Didi, both volunteers, had come to Gautam Nagar near Mahalaxmi Racecourse, begging mothers to send their children to study at their centre. In a few years, it was the mothers who were pleading for their children to be taken into Akanksha! Today, admissions to BMC schools have to be done through a lottery system and the longest queues are outside the Akanksha-BMC schools!

My sister, Deepali, was 3 years old and I was 8 when we got admission in the Akanksha Centre at Rajasthani Mahila Mandal School on Forjet Street. Rumana Didi's warm welcome surprised me—I was not used to strangers being nice! I was immediately accepted as part of the class and that spontaneous acceptance made me feel wanted and secure.

I was never very good in academics. The BMC school I went to had fifty-eight children in a class, but even if we had been five, the teacher would not have noticed or cared about us. I sat on one of the last benches—holding on to a small notebook that I always carried in my plastic bag, not knowing what was happening in class, feeling completely lost. I don't remember learning anything. The didis at the Akanksha Centre, seeing that the school was not right for me, transferred me to another one.

The new school was a big improvement, but I did not do better in class. I was 15 when I cleared Class 8, but my best friend, Mohair Ali, failed, and the teacher announced that he had failed because of my bad influence on him. I was humiliated, and no longer motivated to go to school, bunked classes and stopped doing homework.

My mother was called in to discuss my poor progress. After she left, the teacher told the whole class that Aai was not my mother but an outsider, whom I had paid to come to school. Now I can look back on that incident with calmness, but at that time I was so shaken up that I wanted to slap the teacher. I had been taught never to talk back to adults, so I just sat and listened. But I had lost my self-respect and refused to return to class. If I was younger, Aai would have pulled my ears and taken me right back to school, but I was 15, and she could no longer do that. Bappa (my father) was, as usual, into his alcohol; he did not care.

After I left school, I just hung out with Mohair, until my parents started nagging me to earn a living, since I was useless at everything else. But Dev Bhaiya persuaded me to study privately, and Shaheen Didi offered me her home to study in. For about a month, I went to Sharma's Classes and studied in Didi's house, but I was just not interested in studies. Shaheen Didi did not get upset. 'Don't worry, we will find something you want to do,' she said in an encouraging way, and my confidence went up a hundred points.

What I really wanted to do was teach children from low-income homes like mine, but Sriram Bhaiya, who is awesome, told me that I had to educate myself before I could help others. It took me six years to do that! I was 22 years old when I attempted the Class 10 exam—Dimple Didi, at the Worli 1 Centre, helped me study and Bhavna Didi, a social worker, gave me emotional support. Bhavna Didi is my best friend, and has seen me through many crises. She has now moved to Sydney, Australia, but we communicate regularly, and I know that even though she is far away, we are still very close.

The day before the first paper of the Class 10 board exam, my father died. As the only son, I was expected to perform his last rites. Bappa had died within 12 hours of being admitted to a government hospital, and according to their rules his death became a police case—his body had to go for a post-mortem. Shaheen Didi arrived at the hospital and told me, 'Baba, your father has gone and he will not return. Don't miss this chance to give your exam—go ahead with it.'

I was totally confused—should I perform my father's last rites or go for the exam? If I went for the exam would I let down my family? If I didn't give the exam, would I have the courage to retake it? As I was trying to find the right answer, Shaheen Didi was talking to Aai. She gently explained and convinced my mother how important this exam was for my future and the family's. Aai had a lot of faith in Didi and even today she tells me, 'You can hurt me, but never hurt Shaheen Didi.'

I took Bappa's body to the Nair Hospital morgue, and the kind police officials allowed me to take the body straight to the crematorium and complete the formal paperwork later. The funeral rituals were done while I was writing the exam. Seeing how upset I was, Bhavna Didi accompanied me to the examination hall and waited there until I had finished. I submitted my paper and was permitted to leave early, to return to the crematorium. I was successful in passing the exam and in 2012 completed my Class 12 through the National Institute of Open Schooling (NIOS). I am now working full-time and studying for the Open University.

In times of crisis, the didis and bhaiyas were always near us. When my 3-year-old sister Deepali fell seriously ill, Rumana Didi took her and my mother to the hospital, helped her with the admission process and stayed with her the whole day. My mother has the greatest love and respect for Rumana Didi. I have not met Didi for a long time, so I got the biggest surprise when she called two years ago, to wish me for my birthday.

My interest in social work began with Akanksha's SLP and there were two incidents that defined for me the true meaning of service. At an SLP retreat in Manav Sadhna in Ahmedabad, Rajshree Didi, who was unwell, suddenly vomited in front of everyone. Before she could begin to feel embarrassed, Shaheen Didi, without any fuss, quickly cleaned up the mess—even the smallest action is service. The second occasion was on the day of my sister's wedding. Rajshree Didi and Dev Bhaiya came with friends and before our guests arrived, they scrubbed the community toilet with phenyl (a strong cleaning liquid), so that our guests could use a clean toilet.

A project on leadership, also at Manav Sadhna, demonstrated that during discussions, leaders emerge naturally, and helpful criticism can lead to positive action. I was surprised to hear some of the students say that I had taken the lead in the project!

It was Jayesh Bhai, in Ahmedabad, who awakened in me a strong desire to devote my life to social service. Inspired by him and our experiences in SLP, my friends and I initiated our first project—the cleaning up of our area. Sumeet, Noor and I removed the garbage that was scattered all over the ground where the community children played. For the next few months the children had a clean area to play in, but although the garbage found its way back, it is still much cleaner than before. More importantly, the clean-up idea spread and has now become a movement, with adults in the community contributing to the expenses. I have discovered that once people know what they can do, they are willing to help.

The Mumbai Marathon is held every January, and one year, the Essar Corporation offered to fund the Akanksha runners. Seema Kamble and I went to explain Akanksha's mission to the Essar staff. Their office is in a lavish bluish glass building opposite my slum community, and I never thought that one day I would be invited to go in. The PR plan also included TV and radio presentations. It was opportunities like these that helped me grow. Essar had also offered a free bicycle to the alumni who ran the 21-km race. Unfortunately, being too skinny and with no stamina, I could only make the 7 km Dream Run with the senior citizens!

The best part of the Marathon experience was meeting Nivedita. She was 15 and I was 18. When her parents heard we were seeing each other, they quickly pulled her out of the Akanksha Centre and we did not meet for four years. We belong to different communities—she is a North Indian, I am Maharashtrian. But her parents' bigger objection was that their only daughter wanted to marry into a much poorer family. They saw me as a good-for-nothing fellow, hanging around the streets without money or a proper job.

One day, after four years, Nivedita called me up and we met again. The moment her parents found out about this, she was put under house arrest! Later, to get her occupied and back on track, they opened a beauty salon for her. My mother did not object to the relationship, but was frightened that if I did not end it, her family might harm me.

We decided to get married without her parents' approval. Every step was planned carefully—Nivedita found her birth certificate and ration card and passed them on to me. On the day of the wedding, four of my friends picked her up from the salon and on motorbikes escorted her to the family court in Bandra, where I was waiting. It was like a suspense Bollywood movie!

My wife is a strong woman and she bravely went through it all. Immediately after the wedding, we went to the police station to inform them that we were married, and she had not been kidnapped! With time, her father and mother have come to accept me; they respect my job as a social worker and don't think Nivedita's choice was so bad! On my salary of ₹26,000, their daughter is well-looked-after. The birth of our daughter, Ananya, two years after our marriage, has made my relationship with her parents closer and stronger.

Nivedita has adjusted to my family and we live with my mother, two younger sisters, my elder sister, her husband and two children. There are ten of us in the same house and, at present, I am the only earning member of the family. Nivedita stopped working after Ananya's birth, but once our daughter is in school, she will work as a beautician. There is not sufficient space at home—the family sleeps in the hall and Nivedita, Ananya and I sleep in the kitchen; and during the monsoon the drain water floods the house and reaches to our knees. I want to move to a better place and have already taken a loan—but I must first get my two younger sisters married. There are also medical bills to pay, and we must save so that Ananya can go to a private kindergarten. Things are tough, but manageable.

My mother holds our family together. She was 15 when she got married and has no formal education, but her management skills are amazing. She looks after the younger children, calmly solves family quarrels, and manages the house expenses with the limited money that she is given. Her daily actions are her values— she never cries for help, quietly fulfils her responsibilities and keeps her sorrows tightly inside her. I too never share my problems or my innermost feelings with anyone. Unfortunately, my mother never thought I was any good, until I gave her all my one-year savings from my salary as a teacher, to spend on my sister's engagement. That was the first time I earned Aai's respect.

Bappa and I never got along. He had a temporary job as a painter at the Mahalaxmi Racecourse, and every month when he got his pay, he ran away and returned home after two or three days—drunk! Moneylenders came to our door, and we often had no food; but he never cared what happened to us. When I grew up, his monthly disappearances stopped. Once, Bappa and I had a big fight—it was about something so serious that even now, so many years later, I can't share it with anyone. After the fight, I never spoke to him again. He died at the age of 50. Now I can judge him better. He made some big mistakes, but in his heart he was a good man, and people at the Racecourse still remember and respect him. He had only studied up to Class 2 but he had a lot of general knowledge, and because his handwriting was good, he used to fill in official forms for his friends.

I have been working as a social worker and School Coordinator at the D.N. Nagar Mumbai Public School for ten years. Rakesh Ghone, Department Manager of social work, is a mentor and friend. Sheetal Murudkar, the school Principal, gives me the freedom to do what I want to do. I am the link between the community, students, parents and the school, and help to build a rapport with the BMC. Sorting out problems that affect the children's education or the health of their family, is an important part of my work. I love what I do—I am strong at community work, have facilitation skills and execute projects well. It is on the academic side that I need help! I am researching open universities, where I can get a Master's in social work.

Parents in slum communities deal with their physical and emotional frustrations by using violence. They suffered when they were young, and they inflict those same punishments on their children. I would never raise my hand on Ananya, but it is a common sight to see children with burns caused by their parents.

There are many stories of children we have been able to help. A 7-year-old girl had 25 per cent burns on her back, caused by diyas (oil lamps) on Diwali. The father was jobless and the family depended on the mother's small earnings. We got her funding from the Karo Foundation and the child underwent plastic surgery at the KEM government hospital. She is happily back at school.

Ten-year-old Mohsin was born with severe congenital defects—deformed face and fingers—and was unsteady on his feet. Schools refused to take him because his appearance scared other kids. Mohsin, who is bright and cute, became an introvert and frightened child. I worked on his case for over a year and fell in love with him. We admitted him to the D.N. Nagar Mumbai Public School (managed by Akanksha) and the Karo Foundation funds the multiple and expensive (running into several lakhs) operations that he needs. Two surgeries are over and four remain to be done. Already Mohsin is more confident in school. Each case requires running around and doing follow-ups, but when I see the results, I know that no other job could give me this kind of complete satisfaction.

I can honestly say that it was the didis and bhaiyas who believed in me—made me what I am today. I have not excelled at anything, but my family is comfortable with no major issues. I may not be a perfect role model but I have had a good influence on the community and my family, and help friends take a better track—they know that I will never let them go hungry. I want to do more, but my job takes up a lot of my time. One day, when I have spare time, I will join a dance or drama class—go up on the stage again! Anything can happen—for one thing is always linked to another.

Ananya, who turned 2 in February 2017, is the centre of my universe. We will give her the best education we can—not in a private school, but in an Akanksha school where she will learn good values with her studies. Later she will go abroad to learn whatever interests her. Her challenges will be different from ours. The traditional expectations from our large family and the community will lead to clashes. She will ask more questions than Nivedita and I did, and we must empower her to find the right answers. She will make us very proud of her—I know she will.

∽

'I love what I do—I am strong at community work, have facilitation skills and execute projects well. I am researching open universities, where I can get a Master's in social work.'

MAHESH MANDARE | AKANKSHA | 1997 TO 2009
BCom, Sydenham College
Store Launch Manager and Beverage Trainer, Mad Over Donuts
Date of Birth: 20 January 1992

MAD OVER COFFEE

I am in love with all aspects of coffee and coffee-making. After two years of junior college I took the HSC examination and taking Caroline Didi's advice, joined Café Coffee Day (CCD) as a part-timer, getting a salary of ₹3,000 per month. I saved all my money to pay for my college fees, and for three years I studied and worked simultaneously. The café was not always crowded, and I kept my books next to the billing counter, studying whenever I found time. I was 17 years old.

I loved my job and worked hard. The fun part of being in this industry was that I got to have coffee whenever I wanted. I drank more than ten cups of coffee a day—a coffee addiction! Now I have reduced my consumption to five cups. At the workplace, my talent and eagerness to learn was noticed by my area manager, and I was asked to be a full-timer. The management said if I worked longer hours, I could grow within the organization and it would be good for my career.

I was studying in Sydenham College, doing a BCom degree in Banking and Insurance. College started at noon and when it ended, I went directly to my workplace and began a nine-hour shift from 5 p.m. to 4 a.m.! During this shift, I was in charge of training the team members.

After a few months, I became the store supervisor and cleared the necessary certification to get promoted to Manager. I must

I Dream Like You

have done well in the operation trainee programme, because my trainer said I was the smartest employee in the programme! In the coffee chain business, the art of coffee-making is called latte art. The company's coffee trainer recognized the skills I had in the various aspects of this art, and I was selected to be coffee trainer for Café Coffee Day.

But dreams can come so close to being realized—and then just slip out of our hands! I was about to get my transfer letter for my new appointment, when it was noticed during an audit that one of my juniors had made a stock-taking mistake that was against company policy. Being the manager of the store, I was answerable and had to resign—my dreams shattered in front of me!

During this time my girlfriend, Noorjahan, left home, as her parents objected to her relationship with me—a non-Muslim. Having resigned from CCD, I was out of work and had little money. Noorjahan and I had nowhere to live. We stayed for a few days at a friend's place in Bengaluru and returned to Mumbai to hunt for jobs. At night-time, I helped Noorjahan study for her second year BA exams, and prepared for my own BCom finals. Our parents did not support us and even friends whom I had earlier lent money to were not willing to help—there seemed to be no one we could trust. This was the worst period of our lives but somehow we both managed to clear our exams.

I found work as a receptionist at My Dentist, but I was determined to follow what had become my passion—the Quick Service Restaurant (QSR) industry. After two months, I joined Mad Over Donuts as a Shift Manager, and set a goal for myself: within two years I would be the Store Manager! This was my dream and I focused on it. But again things went wrong. Returning home from work at 4.45 one morning, two guys grabbed and stabbed me in the chest. I was hospitalized for one and a half months and although the company allowed me to rejoin, there were rumours among the staff that I did not deserve to be taken back. I had lost respect and my reputation. I worked as hard as I could until my area manager regained confidence in me.

Finally, I was transferred to the store at Linking Road in Bandra. When the store's monthly sales increased by lakhs of rupees, I was given charge of two more stores, and later transferred to the owner's favourite—at Breach Candy, South Mumbai. When I took over as manager of the Breach Candy store, sales were not up to company standards, and it was my responsibility to increase them.

This was a big honour! Using the prescribed recipe chart, I trained the staff to mix new hot and cold beverages—with and without coffee—willingly sharing my knowledge with trainees.

It was time for my promotion to the position of Store Manager when I made a huge mistake. I carried forward the 'un-topped' donuts for the next day—something that was against standard operating procedure. The result: a warning letter and no promotion! Once more, I had to start from the beginning to prove myself. Fortunately, in the next appraisal I was promoted to Store Manager—one of the most satisfying moments of my life.

Beverages sell less than donuts, cupcakes and cookies, and the aim of the store, and my job, was to encourage customers to buy at least one drink per order. Sales increased, my work was appreciated by the manager and team members, and I soon became a known face in the company. I want to be a role model for my team. Listening to other people's problems and trying to understand their needs, I have developed patience and am able to control my anger.

The recognition I have received all over India is a result of the opportunities that the management has given me. Pramod Valmiki, my area manager, encouraged me to excel, and Santosh Kamble, my previous manager, showed me the importance of being calm and polite with team members. Both of them keep pushing me to learn more and maintain the company's high standards. I try not to let them down.

Considering the job pressure I had, I did not feel fairly compensated compared to the current Quick Service Restaurant market, and decided to move on to another company and a better pay packet. I submitted my resignation, and on my last working day, the owners offered me the designation of a Store Launch Manager and Beverage Trainer. Both Reena Ma'am in the HR department and Shubhankar Sir played a huge role in this appointment. The goal I had set for myself was achieved!

Pooja came into my life four years ago. She used to work in the same organization and has been beside me in the ups and downs of my career. Now she is a Chef De Partie in a small bakery, Pooja makes beautiful cakes and has a good knowledge of bakery products. We are going to get married soon and our parents are happy for us.

Thirteen years of my life—a very long time—were spent at Akanksha, and on every important occasion my actions are influenced by what I learnt there. Our teachers lived by their values—kindness, honesty and hard work. Students understood that without discipline, you go nowhere. But it was the strong

English skills we were taught that will have the biggest impact on my future

One of the best things that happened to me at Akanksha was meeting Caroline Didi—the person closest to me in my life. We travelled together every day to the Worli 1 Centre, talking about different things—personal and related to studies. When I was going through a bad time, she helped me deal with the problem and come back to my regular life. The Centre had many special teachers, but Dimple Didi, Uma Didi and Amrita Didi were extra special. It was also at the Worli 1 Centre that I met Nikhil and Vrukshali, both students, who have become my closest friends. Whatever I say about Akanksha can never be enough—nor can it be expressed in words. Shaheen Didi does not know me by face, but I am so grateful to the organization she started, and maybe, one day, when she walks into one of my stores, I will thank her.

Like all my Akanksha friends, I come from a simple family. Baba, my father, has been the backbone of our family and always supported our studies. He was from a village in Raigarh, Maharashtra, and like so many migrants, came to Mumbai to start a new life—earn money and find a job. He had to leave school in Class 9, because his older brothers had family responsibilities and could not support him through school. His first job was as a labourer, repairing roads, but for the past twenty-five years my Baba has been a gardener, taking care of the gardens of the Taj Mahal Palace, one of Mumbai's most beautiful hotels. He is very knowledgeable about flowers, plants and different types of soil.

Aai (my mother) had a full-time job as a housemaid with a family in the defence forces. We were lucky that her job came with living quarters. Our home was in the army area—near the sea, with trees and plants; calmer, cleaner and more relaxing than the rest of the city. People who lived around us came from a good background, and this helped Baba and us kids to stay away from bad company. Aai never had a proper education and only spoke Marathi, yet she has managed to stand by Dad in all aspects of life—helping with our school fees, clothes and house expenses. She is my inspiration.

We are a family of five and I am right in the middle. My elder brother has been working in the laundry department of the Taj Hotels for over ten years and Ganesh, the youngest, who was also in Akanksha, graduated in Information Technology from HR College and is now with Infosys in Mysore.

My childhood was not fancy. There was always some food, but often dinner had to be divided and eaten at two meals. Baba tried to satisfy our needs in the best way he could. On Sundays, I went crab fishing with him, and crab was our Sunday lunch and dinner.

We had to leave our home when I turned 18, because the Defence Ministry did not give accommodation to children over 18 years of age. We moved to a house that we had in Wadala, which is crowded and dirty and I try to stay away from the young people in that community as much as possible, spending most of the day at work and returning late at night.

My upcoming goal is to be a District Manager and continue training. The day I was made Store Launch Manger and Beverage Trainer, I booked a one-bedroom/hall/kitchen (1 BHK) flat for my family in Virar. It was a double celebration! The builder said that at 24, I was the youngest flat owner in his building, which makes me proud of myself. To own a flat has been one of my biggest dreams—it was always in my head while I was achieving the smaller ones; it was always in my head, while I was having a cup of coffee!

∾

'The builder said that at 24, I was the youngest flat owner in his building, which makes me proud of myself. To own a flat has been of my biggest dreams; it was always in my head while I was achieving the smaller ones.'

SANA ANSARI | AKANKSHA | 1997 TO 2007
Art Assistant, Art for Akanksha
BA final year
Date of Birth: 18 September 1989

LOVE IS EVERYTHING

I was 4 years old when our house burned down. Heena, my 2-year-old sister, was asleep inside and Ammi, my mother, had gone out having locked the house and leaving the key with a neighbour. Luckily, the neighbour was close by when the fire started, and she ran in and pulled my sister out of the flames. In the confusion that followed, Heena wandered away and we found her after many hours. I was at school when the fire broke out and when I returned, there was running and screaming everywhere—people trying to save cooking pans, clothes, mattresses, anything they could pull out from their burning homes. My mother's jewellery and whatever savings we had were gone—we had nothing left. But yes, God was with us, and nobody in our family was hurt.

My Nani and Nana (mother's parents) took us to their home in Vashi but Ammi refused to leave. That night, she slept outside the half-burnt house, afraid that she might lose that too. It all happened in 1994—twenty-four years ago, but my mother talks about it as if it was yesterday.

After one month, when things were settled, we returned home and started our life all over again. It was a big struggle because we had no money, and there were days when we were so hungry and unhappy, that my parents wondered how they would bring up a family in such difficult conditions. But we loved each other a lot and that helped us bear the hardships.

My mother is a housewife but she made some money stitching sequins on saris. She brought the embroidered saris from the karkhanas (workshops) and the four of us—my mother, brother, sister and me—would spread the six-yard material across the floor of our room and stitch on shiny coloured sequins. Ammi got paid ₹100 for each sari, which was a big sum for us.

My father made women's footwear in the Madanpura area of Mumbai. Now he is into retail—he picks up chappals from there, and for a small commission, distributes them to shops. Unlike most men in our area, he has no addictions—he is not into alcohol and does not smoke or chew gutkha.

Like most children in the community, we were regularly beaten by our parents. Sometimes it was for a good reason, sometimes not. Once, mother hit me when I lent my schoolbooks to my friend Nimisha, and then she complained to my teacher, who beat me again! We got used to these physical punishments, and now I understand that it was a way for our parents to let out their own frustration.

Ammi and Papa had studied in Urdu-medium schools until Class 5 only, but they wanted their children to learn English, and we were put in the afternoon shift of an English-medium BMC school. The annual school fees for my brother, sister and me were ₹2,000 and Papa could never get together that large an amount before the due date. Every time he missed the date for payment, my teachers insulted me in front of the class, 'Paise nai hai, to kyu school ata' (If you don't have money why do you come to school?) I could not be angry with Papa, for I saw how hard he worked to feed his large family, but I would wonder, 'Why is education not free, so that everyone can learn happily?' (Later, my two younger siblings went to a free school run by Mukhtangan, an NGO.)

We were much poorer than the other students and Ammi had no money to make me a snack for school, so during recess, when the other students went out to eat, I pretended to work and stayed in the classroom. During the monsoons we could not afford raincoats, and when I arrived at school dripping wet, I had to sit outside in the passage for hours—until my clothes were dry enough for me to enter the class. I was the poor girl from the slum!

I kept to myself and hesitated to make friends. Although it was an English-medium school, no one spoke in English, and the students used the worst Hindi swear words. My classmates thought I was weird and stayed away from me—all except Arti. Arti had a deformity in her fingers and I guess that embarrassed her and kept her away from other children. We both sat on the last bench and became friends. Today she is a data operator and we still keep in touch. I try not to think about my humiliating experiences at school, but it is not easy to forget them, and I question the unfairness in our world. The situation in BMC schools today is supposed to be better—I often wish that I was born in this generation.

The Nehru Planetarium in Worli stands at the entrance of our Mariamma community. The slum spreads from the Planetarium, along the side of Mahalaxmi Racecourse, up to the Nehru Science Centre. Even though the Planetarium was so near to us, we never had the money to buy tickets to go inside, but when some aunty told my mother that a free tuition class had started in that building, I thought, *theek hai* (that's good), 'let's go and see it.'

A curving staircase took us to a large classroom—the Akanksha Centre. There were other children from my community but I did not dare speak to them, for if my mother heard that I talked in class, she would beat me when I got home. I sat quietly in the last row.

The two hours passed quickly. We were taught poems, sang songs, played games and given a free snack of vada pao. At home we were never allowed to do masti (mischief), but here we played around and yet *koi kisiko chilla nahi raha tha* (no one was shouting at anyone). For me, it was a dream world; like coming to another planet! We learnt English, maths and good values and got our general knowledge on field trips to places like Marve beach and Matheran—a hill station. My work was praised; I was the narrator in a play; and when a visitor came to our Centre, I was chosen to give the thank you speech. Sana was no longer the 'weird poor girl'!

At Akanksha, the teachers were called didis. If I had dared call a teacher at the municipal school, didi, she would have slapped me! Rajshree Didi, my first teacher, had a fair complexion, like the dolls I saw in the toy shops—I could not stop looking at her! The best thing about her was that she really believed that if I wanted to do something, I could do it. Soon, I discovered for myself that she was right!

Daphne Didi taught me when I was transferred to the King George Memorial Centre. She was Catholic and sweet and looked the prettiest when she wore her brown trousers and green woollen T-shirt-sweater. Whenever I did not do well in a test, she patiently explained my mistakes, and gently pushed me to do better.

Akanksha was what I imagined heaven to be, and for ten years I was part of this heaven. Around me were people who loved me, and the hugs and kisses I got was something I had never experienced before.

Every field trip we took was fun and taught us a lesson. During the Ganpati Puja festival, we went to the Happy Home and School for the Blind, and I ate the prasad that was given to me by a blind student. My Muslim friends angrily came up to me and said, 'Why did you eat the Hindu prasad? You are a Muslim!' I thought it was polite to eat what was offered, but after their taunts, I began to have doubts...would Allah punish me for eating the prasad? I actually puked, got feverish, kept thinking that God was upset with me. I was frightened to go home, knowing Ammi would be furious. But her response surprised me, 'Don't think like that,' she said gently, 'you will be fine.'

I was still emotionally agitated and feverish when I went to the Centre the next day and met Shaheen Didi for the first time. Looking very concerned, she asked, 'Are you okay?' 'No, I am not,' I replied. She sat beside me and put her hand gently on my forehead—I felt so much better. Today I would gladly accept the prasad, for, although I fast during Ramzan, read the Quran and am proud to be a Muslim, I know that all religions deserve respect.

The biggest setback and disappointment in my life was when I failed my Class 10 exam. As soon as I saw the results on the school board, I wept for hours—tears streaming down my face. In spite of teachers who had mocked me and bad school experiences, I could have done better. My parents wanted me to continue my education, and for one and a half years, Dimple Didi and Dev Bhaiya and Sriram Bhaiya tried to persuade me to retake the exam. But I was demotivated; it would be useless to try again—I could never pass the exam.

I wanted to be left alone; but my didis and bhaiyas did not go away. They came to my house regularly and finally I went back to the Centre. Dimple Didi and Jhanvi Didi helped me in economics, English, business studies and home science. I was 17 when I finally cleared the NIOS exam with 56.5 per cent. The first big hurdle was over.

The only way I could continue studying was to also find work to support the family. Ruchi Didi hired me as an Art Assistant at the Akanksha Art Shop and later I got promoted to Art Associate. The art store sells products made by Akanksha students—beautiful gift bags, paintings, table mats, scarves, trays, etc. Ruchi Didi became a loving mother figure, and four years ago when I was sick with terrible pain and stomach ulcers, she immediately took me to Dr Bela and paid for all the tests. Gauri Didi referred me to a specialist, and three months after his treatment, I was fine. The moment I am happy I glow, if I am stressed I fall ill.

Akanksha had given me a scholarship for the NIOS exam but once I started earning it was not fair to ask for more financial aid. My hard-working mother paid for my tuition and exam fees from her earnings, and two years later I passed the HSC Maharashtra board exam. I was eager to go to a real college but I don't have the brains and I could not afford the fees. Studying independently, with sociology and psychology as my major subjects, I appeared for the BA exam in April 2016 but did not clear it.

Just two days before the exam, Papa had felt giddy at work, and when my brother Aslam went to the station to pick him up,

LOVE IS EVERYTHING

he was sitting against a pillar and could not walk. He did not recognize Aslam and at home he kept looking around the house in a strange manner—a vacant look on his face. I was scared and kept crying but Ammi was super strong. She treated him as she always did, not wanting him to feel frightened or different.

Papa believed in home remedies and had never been to a doctor. We thought it was a mental problem and forced him to see a psychiatrist at Masina Hospital. But he had had a stroke and though he needs to see a neurologist, Papa refuses to go. He has some good days and then forgets everything again. I want him to stop working and tell him I can manage, but he is not ready to listen to my mother or me. Every morning, he goes off to work and I pray he returns safely.

Ammi said I failed the BA exam because my father fell ill but I don't want to make excuses for myself—maybe I was not prepared for the exam. I will definitely do my BA next year and when I get the results, the first person I will call is Sriram Bhaiya, and tell him I have completed my education! After that, no more studying or examinations!

Inspired by my Akanksha didis, an early ambition was to be a teacher—to give children good learning experiences and not be humiliated as I was in the BMC school. During vacations, I made a heavy back-to-back schedule—teaching from 9.30 a.m. to 5.30 p.m. in three different centres. After some time, I could not take on the responsibility of shaping the future of a class of fifty children, and gave up teaching.

Working in the Akanksha Art Shop, I discovered new strengths. In the three years that I have been in the store, I've coordinated with clients and vendors, updated the product database, conducted corporate workshops and sent mailers—all responsibilities that go with managing a small enterprise.

Sriparna, my teacher at work, taught me the procedures for costing, proposal estimates and purchase orders. Handling crisis deadlines and customer complaints was also part of the job, and this was not always easy! A client once screamed at me because her order was not delivered. I was upset by her rudeness, but apologized at once, working overtime to get the order to her as soon as possible. After delivery, I called to recheck if the order was according to her specifications—thankfully, it was! This incident was a lesson in patience, quick thinking and pushing my ego down.

People gossip and say it is time I settled down and had children, but my parents are open-minded and trust me to choose my own husband. When I marry, it will be a Muslim guy, because I think adjustments are easier if you are from the same religion. It is difficult to meet boys within the community but if I were to agree to an arranged marriage, I know that many rishtas (proposals) will come in!

I daydream that one day I will marry a bungalow-wallah (one who owns a house)—a man who is educated, financially well-off, and will always love me. It would be nice to lead a lavish life with my dream boy. But he must understand that after marriage, I will continue working and won't be satisfied being only a housewife. People say I am proud and have a lot of attitude, but there are bad elements in the slum where we live, and I purposely act aloof, so the boys who hang around there stay away from me. At present I am really happy with my life and enjoy the freedom I have to work and do what I please.

Papa does not say much or expresses his emotions, but when any of us falls ill he gets very worried. Once my mother had gone out for just a short while, and Papa stayed with me, refusing to go to work until she returned. My mother is amazingly broad-minded, expresses her feelings openly and gives each of us the space to do what we think is best. My younger sister wears a burqa when she goes out. Neighbours tell Ammi that I should wear one too, especially because I am older than my sister—but I never do. I go out in jeans with a long kurta, but am not permitted to wear skirts and blouses. I accept some restrictions because there are unruly loafer boys who roam our area.

It has not been easy for Ammi to adapt her conservative ideas to her children's modern lifestyle. When we go to my father's village in Raja ki Mandi, Agra, relatives are critical of the freedom we have, finding us too frank in our speech. My mindset is very different from the girls in the village, most of whom have never been to school, and are married by the age of 17 or 18. So I don't interact with anyone, and just pass my time, waiting to come home. My Nana and Nani are traditional and deeply religious, yet they accept me for who I am. I have the happiest time in their home, sitting around, just being with them.

My biggest challenge has been studying for the Class 10 exam and working at the same time. Most of my salary goes to Papa and Ammi, and now we have enough to buy new clothes for Eid, and not worry about food. On special occasions, we go out for dinner to Persian Darbar and Nooranis, and often have snacks at Hotel Sadanand. My two younger siblings won't have the same poverty issues that I did.

We have a *pukka cement ka ghar* (proper house made of cement), and don't live in a *patray ka ghar* (house of tin sheets), like we did earlier. Unfortunately, there is still no indoor toilet because drainage pipes have not been laid out in our area of the community. One day I will earn lots of money and convince Ammi to move out to a 3 BHK or even a 4 BHK flat! She says, '*Mujhay jana nahi*' (I don't want to leave), but one day I know she will change her mind. Until then, we follow Ammi's valuable advice: '*Jitna hai utnay mein hi khush rahene ki koshish karni chahiye*' (try to live happily within your means).

My parents pushed us to study and this has brought them good results. My brother, Aslam, is a graduate and works as a tea sommelier at Basilur; Heena studied till Class 10, and is now learning tailoring; and my youngest siblings are in the Mukhtangan school. With my brother and me earning, we live comfortably, and our status in the community has risen. Neighbours, who once ignored us because we were poor, now praise my parents for educating their children. It is sad but true, that when you have money, people are nicer to you.

After I get my BA degree, I must test myself in the outside world. I will look for a bigger job in sales and marketing where I can meet new people and compete on deadlines. I am a Salman Khan fan and my first choice will be working in the main office of his NGO, Being Human Foundation—20 per cent because of him, and 80 per cent because it is a good organization.

We are often told to look back and learn from our past experiences. My memories at the BMC school were so traumatic that I only want to look forward, to move ahead—'*chhota chhota*' (tiny, tiny) steps at a time.

∞

'With both my brother and me earning, we live comfortably, and our status in the community has risen. Neighbours, who once ignored us because we were poor, now praise my parents for educating their children. It is sad but true that when you have money people are nicer to you.'

HUSSAIN SAYYED | AKANKSHA | 1994–1996, 2008–2010, 2012–2014

BSc Biology, St Xavier's College, Mumbai

MA, Public Policy

Programme Leader, Kaivalya Education Foundation

Piramal Foundation Award for Best Initiative, 2016

Gandhi Fellowship, Kaivalaya Education Foundation, 2012

Date of Birth: 4 August 1989

TRANSFORMING LEARNING SPACES

Somewhere along the way I realized that I was the hero of my life. I had to be my own leader. If I wanted something to be done, I had to do it. It was Shaheen Didi who made me see the many possibilities in myself.

My roots are in a large family. We are four siblings and today ten of us live together—my parents and grandmother; my brother, his wife and their two children; my sister and her daughter; and me. Our home is one room at Dana Bunder, near the famous Chhatrapati Shivaji Terminus (CST) railway station in Mumbai. Growing up in a crowded tin-roof room in a crowded slum, I didn't think I had many options, and there was never the time and space to sit alone and plan for better things.

Apa, my father, left school in Class 7. He worked in a shipping hardware store and earned a salary of ₹1,500–2,000 per month. Gradually he became lazy, and for the past ten years instead of going to work, he totally occupies himself looking after the Durga Devi temple next to our house—and supervising the temple's Trust matters. Ma is Muslim. Apa, a Hindu converted to Islam, but follows his own God. Mixed marriages are still not welcome in our society and my parents must have faced big difficulties when they got married. It's perhaps because he is so obsessed with religious rituals that although I follow Islam, I don't always practise my religion.

Ma studied only till Class 2, and all these years, she has put in hard work, picking out little stones and dirt from baskets of raw rice and wheat and selling the cleaned grain. She has been the one who has earned and got us food—Apa contributed very little to our expenses. Ma's love, no matter what I did, has been my greatest support and she is the most important person in my life.

Apa helps people fight for their legal rights, especially when slum redevelopment projects force them to leave their homes. Ma feels that everyone takes advantage of him, and he should spend time providing for his family—this leads to fights between them. Sometimes I think Apa's need for attention is greater than his desire to help people!

My three older siblings—Laila, Rasul and Hasan—studied Tamil in a BMC school, but father wanted me to go to a good English school, and enrolled me in St Ignatius, where the ₹125 monthly fees was affordable. After four years, I transferred to Sir JJ Fort Boy's High School. I was a very average student until Class 10 and did not make good use of the school, but enjoyed extracurricular responsibilities, and was a member of the Student Council.

Teachers can impact their students both positively and negatively. In Class 10, my class teacher, Pressena Pillai, made me the House Captain and my confidence soared! But it came crashing down when I scored 45 per cent in the preliminary examinations. For the first time I took charge of myself, put in 100 per cent effort, studied the hardest I ever had, and scored 76 per cent in the board finals. I was a topper in social science, and got admission to St Xavier's College, a premier institution in Mumbai.

To be a 'Xavierite' was a big deal for me. I had first entered the college as an Akanksha student, when I was 5 years old. The Foundation conducted after-school classes in the lecture rooms on the ground floor of the college, and sitting in class I imagined myself all grown-up—walking into St Xavier's as a proper college student.

The Akanksha Centre was my first experience in a class, and I stayed at the Centre until I was 12 years old. For one or two years I could not attend regularly because the timings of the Centre clashed with my regular school and tuition class. But every time I came back, I loved it.

At the Centre we learnt without punishment. I cherished this the most, because in my previous school even if a few kids misbehaved, everyone got a beating. It was an unfair system and I became fearful of the beatings that became a part of the class curriculum! The teachers—didis and bhaiyas—were the heart and soul of our classrooms. There was a simplicity about them, and their eyes sparkled when they read aloud from the biographies of great men and women. The heroes in those books became my role models, and I was inspired to set goals for myself. Writing down our reflections, a regular class activity, made us aware of our strong and weak points. I grew a little wiser after every class.

My college years at St Xavier's were happy ones, but I had few friends. There was a social gap between me and the students who came from higher-income families. I felt awkward with my peers, although, I must admit, I am an introvert and did not put any effort into making new friends. My friends today are those I knew at school and at Akanksha.

It had been a secret aspiration of mine to become a doctor,

I Dream Like You

and after passing junior college, I wanted to study medicine. Illness and disease are common in our community, and I know that many people would have recovered faster and better if they had proper medical attention. I saw myself healing those who could not get to the hospital on time. I did get admission in a private medical college, but could not put together the money to pay the fees and so stayed on at St Xavier's, and graduated with a BSc in Biology—a subject I love.

As a child, I was curious to find out how and why everything worked the way it did. Why did certain fruits appear at certain times of the year? How did the water on earth become the rain that fell from the sky?

A magician, who had once come to perform in the slum, demonstrated a trick where he poked a long thin needle into a balloon, and the balloon did not burst! Curious why the balloon did not burst, I went to the Internet and found the answer—the pressure is lower at the point you tie the balloon, than it is at the opposite end, and if you stick the needle through these two points, the balloon does not burst!

Hundreds of questions came to my mind, and sometimes, I found the solutions many years later. When we were children, my granny had a strange way of 'taking away' the nazar (evil eye) from us. She set fire to small pieces of paper, put them in a glass, and turned the glass over a plate of water. After a few seconds, the water in the plate rose up into the upturned glass. She believed it was magic but I knew there had to be another explanation. When I was older, I discovered that the burning paper uses up the oxygen in the glass. Once the flames die and there is no oxygen there is space in the glass for the water to rise! I experimented in the college laboratory and discovered some of the solutions myself. Chess definitely helps me to work out strategies. A friend and I picked up the game watching my uncles play, and in school and college I participated in chess tournaments at the district level.

I was 17 years old when I was selected for the Akanksha LTL programme—a two-year part-time course for academically smart students. We studied national and world events; debated social, financial and political issues; and researched individual projects. In those two years, I honed my skills, got confidence and travelled to different places across the country.

We were taken to Infosys in Bengaluru; we interacted with the senior staff at Mahindra and Mahindra and the Taj Hotels Group; we saw the work done on governance at the NGO, Praja; and studied the methods Pratham uses to fight illiteracy in India. I learnt how corporations adapt and meet their goals, how different leaders overcame obstacles and how issues must be examined from different perspectives. Above all, my experiences at LTL gave me the tools to dream big.

I joined Akanksha's SLP to pass the time on Sundays but realized very fast that it was much more than 'timepass'. The SLP was about social service and developing decision-and-leadership skills. Mansi Didi led our training sessions and everything she said came straight from her heart. I remember her advice, 'When you are happy, laugh out loud, and when you are sad, cry out aloud. That way, you will always keep space in your heart for the next feeling.' Rohit Bhaiya, SLP's most outspoken teacher, was aggressive in a positive way and pushed us to our outermost limits, building confidence so that we never saw ourselves as 'underdogs'.

Every project at SLP was organized with a purpose. A

presentation to the Board members of Thermax; and an Asia Society seminar on women's rights, where I shared the stage with actor and activist Rahul Bose and Mr A.N. Roy, then the police commissioner of Mumbai, improved my speaking skills and confidence. After Harish Iyer's session on transvestites and sexual abuse, I became sensitive to issues that I had earlier paid no attention to.

There was one experience in particular that I will not forget. We visited a home for destitute women in Govandi where women had been repeatedly raped by government officers on official visits. The media had reported the incident and the case was in all the newspapers. The poor women were so traumatized that they could not bear to see, or be seen by men! I felt such anger at the injustice done to these women, and from that day on, I understood the importance of fighting for women's rights.

Looking back on my childhood, I realized that gender discrimination was practised in my own home! I always ate dinner before my sisters; I never washed utensils or did household chores that they were required to do. I grew up thinking that was the way everyone lived! The Govandi visit forced me to re-examine my beliefs. I did not have to be a doctor to serve those in need; I could choose my own route for service, I could be my own NGO.

It is the little things that change one's life. Mine was completely transformed by meeting a young boy in the Dharavi Crosswords School No. 2. Locals called it the 'khadda school' because it looked like a hole or den! When we visited the school, it was in a pathetic condition—peeling paint, leaking toilets, broken chairs, etc. But more depressing than the building were the children inside it. The students walked around with no energy, looking unhappy and frightened. I asked one of the boys sitting around why he had come to this school and he gave me an honest reply: '*Kyun ki main garib hoon*' (because I am poor). He said he would like to go to a 'private school' with bright lights, pictures on the walls and washbasins that had running water in the bathrooms. I jotted down the boy's list of wishes, and spent the next two months working to get money to repair his school.

Many people volunteered to donate towards the renovations but they wanted an 80G certificate for tax deduction and since mine was not a registered NGO, I could not officially do this. I sent emails to a hundred people, and after the first donation of ₹250, the money kept coming in... Soon, we had collected ₹1.2 lakh, with the school staff contributing ₹10,000 towards the repairs as part of their Ramzan Zakat (a donation given during the Muslim fasting month).

A hired contractor completed the basic repairs and put the base coat of paint on the walls. But then we ran out of money! The teachers at the school contributed again and we bought more paint. On a Sunday morning, with a group of St Xavier's students, I went to the school with tins of paint in bright colours and brushes of different sizes. By evening, there were paintings all over the classroom walls—familiar and unfamiliar fruits and vegetables to increase vocabulary, vertical scales encouraging children to measure their own heights, simple diagrams showing the different angles of doors and windows, as they open and close.

On Monday, my little friend entered his 'private school'. It had yellow, red and green classrooms, pictures on repaired walls, new electric wiring and bright lights. The renovation worked like magic, and the khadda school, which no one wanted to go to, now has a long queue of parents waiting to pick up admission forms.

The boy's name is Karim and his dream became my dream. With the help of a few friends, I went on to transform fifteen other broken-down schools into fun-and-creative-learning environments. In Rajasthan, the amazing project, Building As Learning Aid (BALA), an initiative of the Sarva Shiksha Abhiyan, demonstrates that like toys and books, architecture too can inspire learning.

Akanksha now runs municipal schools with hundreds of children, and the centres that I knew, are no more. I am definitely not happy about this. The flexible curriculum at the Centre gave teachers the freedom to share their passions with students and there was always time to discuss topics after class. We were taught in small groups and field trips became exciting experiences. Change is necessary and important, but I hope that many of the qualities that made the centres so special, will also become a part of the Akanksha-managed BMC schools.

After graduating from St Xavier's College in 2012, I applied for the Gandhi Fellowship at the Kaivalya Education Foundation, founded by Aditya Natraj. There were applicants from all over India for the two-year residential training course, and for the first time, I was competing in the real world. I was lucky to be accepted for the fellowship, and the two years I spent there transformed my thought process, and gave a purpose to my life.

We learnt how to interact with parents, children and school leaders—the roots of every school tree. We intervened with the community, talked to counsellors and worked on systems and processes that improved the learning in schools. As part of the training, I was given independent responsibility for five schools—and that is where I found the hero in myself.

I am now a Programme Leader at Kaivalya Education Foundation, and I mentor the Fellows in the programme—coordinating between the Foundation, schools, communities and government education officers. Our focus is to observe and research on how children can learn best—transferring the attention from teacher to student. The strong values at the Kaivalya Education Foundation, aligned to my own value system, make it an ideal place for me to work; all evaluations and impact studies are presented with honesty, even if the numbers don't show the results we aimed for.

In 2015, I engaged with 300 Foundation staff members and we worked for sixty-five days to transform learning spaces in twenty schools. During this period, I also interacted with fifteen other schools, where the staff became stakeholders, and together we renovated their institutions. For this work, I received the Piramal Foundation Award for the Best Initiative.

Lopa Didi from Akanksha is a consultant at the Foundation, and I feel proud that at meetings, we sit side by side as colleagues. At 27, I am the youngest in the organization, and there is a lot more that I need to learn, especially about resource mobilization and marketing. Recognizing that I am not as well read as some of my colleagues who have been to better private schools, I try to gain knowledge through books and educational videos. When my college generously contributed towards my fees, and my brother who is a sports coach in a school and privately studying for the Class 12 exam, could support the family, I left the Foundation to be a full-time student.

In 2017, I completed my Master's in Public Policy from

St Xavier's, a degree that will qualify me for more responsible jobs in public service. I don't want to be the richest person in the world, but I want to make a worthwhile contribution— keeping a smile on the face of kids like Karim is one goal, taking responsibility to see that my family is well and healthy is another. My mother never had much, and even today, she doesn't expect life to give her anything. I want her to be just a housewife and do nothing, but she says that only when she feels financially secure will she stop working.

Many years ago, I did not believe Shaheen Didi when she said that each one of us has unlimited potential, and every child can get an education. In a country where 90 per cent of the children drop out before Class 5, her dream seemed like an impossible task. Today my dreams are big too, though perhaps not as big as hers! I remember reading somewhere, 'Work on your own private dreams, or someone will make you work for their dreams.' Nothing has come easily to me, and I need to put in maximum effort for my own dreams to work out—dreams of hundreds of brightly painted schools and thousands of smiling children running into them.

⟶

'There were applicants from all over India for the two-year residential Gandhi Fellowship training course, and for the first time, I was competing in the real world. I was accepted for the fellowship, and the two years I spent there transformed my thought process and gave my life a purpose.'

MAHESH LONDHE | AKANKSHA | 1999 TO 2008
BCom, Brihan Maharashtra College of Commerce
Chartered Accountant
Senior Executive: Corporate Finance, Legal and Taxation Division, Thermax
Date of Birth: 24 July 1993

THE POWER OF AN ENTREPRENEUR

I was 15 years old when I stopped to look into a car showroom not far from our house. The cars were lined up, their colours bright and shiny—red, gold, blue and silver. As soon as I got home, I ran to my parents and asked, 'Can we buy a four-wheeler?' Papa was quick to reply, 'We can't afford it.' And I quickly killed the thought that we could ever own a car.

Years later, I wondered what my reaction would have been if Papa had said, 'Think about how we can afford it.' It would have put pressure on me to think of alternatives, and in my enthusiasm, I would have worked out different ways we could have saved and bought a car. It was much later that I understood the value of creative thinking. Most schools do not encourage children to explore possibilities. In fact, kids today are programmed not to think freely. The Akanksha Centre was an exception.

I was 5 years old when I first sat in an Akanksha classroom. The children were the focus here—in and out of the class. Questions were encouraged, there was no mugging up of lessons, and when we made mistakes, we just tried again. There was always somebody in the room who cared about what we did or said. Everything seemed different here; everything was special here. The Centre was not perfect and there was scope for improvement, but the teachers were not hardcore traditional, and they tried to create a holistic learning experience.

Our didis were blind to colour, gender or caste. Teachers, students, the bai who swept the rooms, the little boy who served chai and the man who cleaned the toilets—each one deserved respect, and at our Centre they got it.

The Mentor Programme for older children was a way to widen our horizons, and it actually worked very well. It was drafted in a perfect way with every student assigned to an individual mentor. I was a shy kid and it was my mentor, Ashish Patki, a soft-spoken engineer, who made me understand the importance of taking initiative and grasping opportunities that came my way. We met for an hour every Saturday—for a short six months. But in that small span of time, he had a great influence on me. He was an excellent listener and helped me with my academic problems and college selections. Bhaiya is now in the US for higher studies.

The Akanksha organization is shutting down the two-hour Learning Centre model and taking over the teaching and management of municipal schools. This is a great initiative, for it gives teachers longer time to work with the students and transform their mindset. More children will now have the opportunity to be taught by dynamic Akanksha didis and bhaiyas. If I had been in an Akanksha six-hour school, instead of a two-hour Centre, how much more could I have learnt!

It is the rote teaching approach in the regular municipal schools that shuts minds and kills ideas. The PMC Bharat English School, where I studied, is only one of hundreds, maybe thousands of schools, where students are not expected to think. The teachers in my PMC school just followed the prescribed syllabus and rules. There was no interaction between students and teachers, and the only way we passed a test was by mugging up textbooks.

I was the first person in my family to clear Class 10, after which I transferred for the next two years to the English-medium Brihan Maharashtra College of Commerce (BMCC). I was ready to embrace college life with open arms, but with college came problems. The studies were difficult and very competitive, for every student in BMCC was a scholar or merit holder! Also, I was socially not at ease with the high-class college crowd and my mini-pocket could not keep up with the expensive habits of other students. I spent most of my time in my own zone—with students whose backgrounds were like mine. And then, I passed my HSC board (Class 12) examination with flying colours. It was a 'wow' moment for the whole family!

I learnt the value of working hard from my father, Mr Vishnu, who is a bhel vendor (bhel is a street snack made with puffed rice) at the Pune railway station. Papa dropped out of school in Class 5, started working at the age of 13, and has never stopped. For 12 to 14 hours a day he is at the station, running onto and jumping off trains—a dangerous way to sell peanuts and bhel! In his own way, Papa is an entrepreneur, selling his snacks wherever he can—climbing onto trains as they slow down, running along the train corridor and standing at the main gate as passengers leave the station. He changes the food items depending on their popularity and enjoys his independence.

Papa once had bigger dreams, but the death of his mother at an early age and the family's poor finances, killed them before they were born. He planted the seeds of his dreams in his three children and is now waiting for us to grow into giant trees. My father is a man with great self-respect, a most dedicated and loving person.

My mother, Mrs Vimal, works as a helper at an Akanksha Centre. On Diwali, Papa and Mummy never spend money on themselves; instead, they buy new clothes for us, saying it gives them joy to see their children all dressed up. My parents are my role models.

Our home in Patil Nagar in Pune is on the bank of the Mula-Mutha River. Almost 1,200 to 1,500 families, practising a mix of all religions live here. We have a small 10 ft × 10 ft home and our family of five fits right into it. Fifty to 60 per cent of the inhabitants of the community are scrap and ragpickers and there is almost no literacy in the age group of 30 and above. Parents now want a better life for their children and the younger generation, realizing the value of education, wants to study and not follow in their parents' footsteps. Akanksha has been the game changer in the community and around 100 children from Patil Estate have been to Akanksha centres. Parents had faith in the organization, and their children's progress convinced them that it was the right place for them to study.

Being the oldest of three siblings, I have always felt a 'role model' responsibility towards my younger brother, Ratnadeep, and sister, Monica; and after passing HSC, I wanted to take on the responsibility of earning for my family. Both my siblings, Akanksha alumni, are also carving out a future for themselves. Monica is in her first year of BCom and attending a beautician's course, while my brother is in the Marathwada Mitra Mandal's College of Commerce (MMCC). Akanksha has motivated us three siblings to create our own three stories.

When I was younger, I had no definite career in mind. I knew

I did not want to be a doctor or an engineer and since I was not strong in mathematics, by a process of elimination, I chose commerce. Then I had the crazy idea to work simultaneously on a CA qualification and a BCom degree. I was ready to knock on the door of success, and the combined support of the career guidance programmes at Akanksha and BMCC, encouraged me in my decision. CA is a very difficult course and everyone tried to dissuade me, worried that not being able to clear the exams, I would end up discouraged and frustrated.

But I was ready to face the music, certain that for me to achieve something big, CA had to be attempted. I had a clear equation in my mind, 5 = 50 (five years of hard work equals fifty years of enjoyment!) My parents backed me 100 per cent, always believing that I could do it.

CA is an expensive course and I knew my father could not afford the fees. Papa already had heavy loans and it was taking years to pay them off. So like many other alumni, I turned to Akanksha.

Anandi Yagnaraman, the new director of Akanksha, Pune, knew nothing about me, but somehow she was convinced of my ability to handle two degrees together, and agreed to help me. She introduced my mother and me to Mrs Anu Aga and Mrs Meher Pudumjee, at Thermax, a big corporation in the business world.

After a long discussion and interview (I was more nervous than Mummy!), they agreed to take my plan forward, on one condition—if I failed in any one of the CA exams, the sponsorship would end. It was a fair deal and I accepted it. Mr M.S. Unnikrishnan, Managing Director of Thermax, generously offered to be my sponsor.

The dual pressure of BCom and CA was tough and has prepared me to face even tougher situations. I graduated with a BCom—one of the top five students on the Pune University merit list, and received two awards. On Prize Distribution Day, Papa and Mummy sat in the audience, their eyes filled with tears—feeling a happiness they could not express in words. Their pride in my achievement pushed me to go on building a successful career for myself. I can never repay them for all the things they have done for me, and now, it is my turn to make them happy.

The CA course was a killer and preparing for the finals was by far the greatest challenge I have ever faced. After completing the Integrated Professional Competency Course (IPCC), which is the second phase of the CA course, I did Articles for three years, getting a monthly stipend of ₹3,000. During this period I was working for my Principal, attending classes and spending many hours studying on my own.

To study at home was not easy. The houses in our locality are close to each other and only separated by thin walls. If someone speaks loudly in a neighbour's house, we can hear everything. And there is a craze for playing music on loudspeakers at a very high volume. Since the neighbourhood remained noisy all day and until late every night, I went to the public library at Prestige Point in Shukrawar Peth. I studied wherever and whenever I could—sometimes on the street in front of Fergusson College.

To make a proper timetable for myself, I tried various permutations and combinations. For the first few months, I worked all night, then shifted to daytime studying, and later to a combination of both. As the exams got nearer, the six to eight hours of daily study increased to fifteen and sixteen hours. I went to the library at 8.30 a.m. and returned home at 3.30 the next morning, slept for four hours, drank a glass of milk, had something to eat, and went back to the library. There was only one goal in front of me—clearing my CA in the first attempt.

The results were declared on 16 July 2015. I woke up early that morning, shut my eyes tight and prayed, 'If I have given 100 per cent effort to this exam, I deserve a 100 per cent result.' At 11.30 a.m., I got the news—I had passed at the first go! My prayers had been answered, my efforts rewarded. The family was thrilled, and the next day I was in the Marathi and English newspapers: 'Son of Pune bhel vendor clears CA Final in first attempt!' The news spread like a wildfire through the shacks of Patil Estate. Journalists came to our house, and on TV there was a small bite on the journey of my life. I was 22 years old and had become a celebrity!

I was no longer part of the audience—I was a showstopper! My success encouraged the girls and boys in our area, 'If a slum community guy can crack the BCom and CA exams in the first try, we can also make it.' Maybe the young people of my community will now set higher goals for themselves.

After my CA, I interviewed again with Thermax, the corporation that had supported my CA studies, but this time it was for a job. I now work in Corporate Finance as a Senior Executive in the Legal and Taxation Division. I am very happy at Thermax, but in the long term I want to be an entrepreneur. I need the independence to explore all the things I want to do; to think of ways that I can afford the car that I saw in the showroom window so many years ago.

Today, I understand the meaning of Gandhiji's words, 'Be the change you want to see in the world.' My interpretation is: Move away from hopelessness and fear and live the world of your dreams. Make yourself capable of changing the world, and then change it. 'Change' is a powerful word—I am starting to acquire the power to 'Be the Change.'

Perfect planning leads to perfect execution. A very small part of my journey has been completed, and there are many challenges ahead—I plan to get an MBA from an Indian Institute of Management or the Indian School of Business and acquire managerial skills and finance-related experiences. Education is the only vehicle to get me to my destination and from 2016 I have begun to study for a law degree.

Working in a corporation and waiting for an annual salary hike of ₹5,000 or ₹10,000 does not excite me. I don't want to spend my whole life in the four walls of an office; I want to create my own world not only for monetary benefit, but also for personal growth and satisfaction. My interest and future lie in finance; maybe I will be a financial consultant on taxation matters and market strategies, or establish an investment company. To build my own empire, I will hire a team of professionals and pay them well. In one of his books, Robert T. Kiyosaki writes, 'Don't work for money, money should work for you.' I aim to create an asset for myself, and, hopefully, money will work for me, and I will not have to wait for a ₹5,000 salary raise!

I want to keep my options open. The desire to serve India comes directly from my years at Akanksha. Sometime in the future, I will prepare for the Union Public Service Commission (UPSC) that will qualify me to become an officer of the India Administrative Service (IAS). And then who knows? I may abandon the financial world and serve India.

The education system in India puts pressure on students to

get a job as quickly as possible. Schools are employee-producing machines and don't encourage entrepreneurship. Students are threatened that the alternative to employment is an eternal struggle. To me, financial literacy means being aware of the various options I have to earn a living—not only job employment. Many of my friends were not aware of these options, and unable to find a job, ended up doing nothing!

In the financial world, Warren Buffet is my hero. He was 10 years old when he started a business of selling chewing gum, newspapers and Coca-Cola; at the age of 11, he had already purchased shares on the New York Stock Exchange. His two rules for success make sense to me—rule no. 1, never lose money; rule no. 2, never forget rule no. 1!

I want to be rich, but with my own efforts. Mr Buffet built Berkshire Hathway from zero—investing wisely, he changed the investment game. Starting from zero, perhaps I too, will bring about changes in the money market. I appreciate the value of every rupee, of hardcore effort, of keeping my feet firmly on the ground.

Mr Buffet wisely said, 'No matter how great the talent or effort, some things take time.' I have the time, for, my story has only begun—'*picture abhi baki hai mere dost!*' (the movie is still to be completed my friend).

∽

'The education system in India puts pressure on students to get a job as quickly as possible. We are threatened that the alternative to employment is an eternal struggle. Schools are employee-producing machines, and don't encourage entrepreneurship.'

SEEMA KAMBLE | AKANKSHA | 1998 TO 2006
BCom, Lala Lajpatrai College of Commerce, Mumbai
Principal, Mahatma Jyotiba Phule Market (MPS) English-Medium School, Mumbai
Teach For India Fellowship programme, 2010
321 Schools, Founding Team Member and Principal
Date of Birth: 27 May 1986

MAKING CHOICES

In 2010, I graduated from the Lala Lajpatrai College of Commerce, and was accepted for an MBA programme at the Welingkar Institute of Management, Mumbai. My parents always wanted their children to study, but an MBA was something beyond their wildest dreams. The degree would transform my family's life, and mine. I would get a good job, earn a big salary, meet interesting and successful people, and visit places I had seen only in magazines.

In that same year I applied to TFI's two-year fellowship programme, teaching in India's most challenging schools. The TFI applicants came from top colleges in India and universities in the US—Harvard, Georgetown and Stanford. Prestigious corporations, including Hewlett Packard, Thermax, Tata Consultancy Services and Mahindra and Mahindra, sent their well-qualified officers. Shaheen Didi, Rajshree Didi and Shveta Didi had convinced me that I could succeed in the programme, and I believed in them. That year, TFI received 3,900 applications and only 7 per cent were accepted. I was one of them.

The TFI training was rigorous and though the stipend was small, after two years, I could help millions of children who go to schools with poor infrastructure, and uncaring, and sometimes cruel, staff. I had been taught by creative and loving teachers; maybe I could pass on what I had learnt, to bridge the educational gap in India. During college, I had worked in Akanksha's PR department, with people who had known and protected me for years. Should I move on and explore the world—be independent and discover myself? Should I stay in India and help reform the education system?

Two life-transforming opportunities were in front of me; I had to make a decision. MBA or TFI? It was a tough choice. I chose Teach For India.

Shaheen Didi, the founder of TFI, was a familiar face from my Akanksha days. Her vision for the organization was daring: 'All children can attain an excellent education and TFI will help to make it happen.' The two years I was a Fellow in TFI were the most challenging ones I have experienced. After the six-week, intensive, residential 'Institute', a team of support staff was with us throughout the two years.

I did my fellowship in Pune, teaching forty children from classes 3 and 4, and the real test began on the very first day—as soon as I walked into the classroom. The kids could not read or write, and barely managed to sit through a class period of forty minutes. My first thought was, 'Can I really cross the wide gap between what they know, and what I want them to learn?' And then I remembered...wasn't I one of these children not so long ago, until someone came and believed in me? The next day, I walked into the same class, confident that I could make a change.

In two years, my forty kids had learnt to read books of Class 4 level and above; performed *Charlie and the Chocolate Factory* in English, in front of 500 people; and debated on the importance of education with representatives of the PMC.

The more I taught, the more I learnt. When a few parents

pulled out their children for one reason or the other, the children fought their way back to school! My students, Aftab and Sania, still keep in touch with me, and we have a close relationship. Their stories, like Pranjal's, have become part of my story.

Pranjal was a girl with eyes that sparkled when she danced or discovered something new. Her confidence was amazing. The students were once asked to write a poem on 'Belief', and this is what 8-year-old Pranjal wrote:

I believe I can become a fairy
I believe I can swim in the water
And fly in the sky
I believe I can dance
I believe I can sing
I believe I can walk like a monkey
And go to the zoo and play with animals
I believe I can draw
I believe I can read
I believe I can become a teacher
I believe I can become a CHAMP!

The Fellows at TFI came from diverse backgrounds, and there was an incredible energy in and out of the classrooms. The course was demanding, and the conditions in the schools we taught in were often terrible, pushing us to find solutions and adapt to difficult situations. A large percentage of fellows who graduated with me have continued in some form of education. Others chose different careers, but will continue to support TFI's mission in their own way.

My early years were spent in a pleasant flat in Navy Nagar, Mumbai, where my grandfather had an Army job, and my mother was a sevika (helper) in the Navy School. Mummy can hardly read or write, but she worked hard all her life to give her children a good education. The Kindergarten Naval School, my first learning environment, had good teachers, and along with academics we had co-curricular activities, like stitching, sports, quilling, art and acting.

When grandfather retired from the Army, we relocated to the nearby Ambedkar Nagar Community, a growing slum along the sea. After the neatness of Navy Nagar, the dirt and violence in the slum came as a big shock. We could not afford a private school, and were sent to a BMC school in Colaba. Teachers entered the class, wrote something on the board for us to copy and then either left the room or sat down and relaxed. I don't remember learning much, and didn't enjoy school at all—always wanting to go back to my previous one.

Three years after we came to Ambedkar Nagar, a fire in the community burned down our house. In the same week, Papa, who used to drink heavily, went to my grandmother's home in Pune for medical treatment. But he never went to the doctor; one day, he just walked out of the house and did not return. We searched everywhere, put ads in the newspaper for months—but we could not find him. We still don't know whether he is alive or dead.

I was only 8 years old when Papa went away but I still think of him. He had passed his Class 10, could read, write and speak English, and he always made sure that we were home before 7 p.m., so that he could take up our studies. He was a heavy drinker and when he drank, he 'lost his mind'. At other times, he was fine.

Mother's life was not easy. Father used to beat her up when

he had too much to drink, and though he did not work most of the year, he demanded that she provide him a luxurious life.

My most joyous moment was when I got a part-time job after Class 12 and took on the family responsibility, so that my mother no longer had to go out to work.

When our house burned down, we relocated to Worli, and for a few months stayed in an unused office room provided by my grandfather, who was now a local corporator. Staying with my grandparents was not a permanent solution, and Mummy found a 10 ft x 10 ft room in the Mariamma Nagar community. Over the years, we started to make improvements in our room by changing the rough cement floor to a tiled one and replacing the patra (tin sheets) with brick walls.

There were water shortages and street fights, and no sanitation facilities. Alcoholic neighbours fought over things that made no sense to me; and girls dropped out of school and became mothers at the age of 15 or 16. I was 10 years old, and I remember crying a lot—disturbed, angry, helpless and numb at what was happening around me. I wanted to run away to a place where I wouldn't see any of these things. But there seemed no choice except to continue seeing and doing what I didn't like.

Homes were regularly demolished by bulldozers of the BMC, who called them relocation projects! Builders make a profit out of slum redevelopment projects by building commercial buildings on community land, and then offering us alternative housing. Five years after we moved to Mariamma, our house was taken over by a builder, and we were given a 1 BHK flat on the seventh floor of a new building, in the same community.

And then there were the good things that happened—Mansi

Didi, Nikki Didi and Dev Bhaiya came to support those whose homes had been destroyed. They prepared food for them in the community temple, and helped them with what they needed.

Moving from Cuffe Parade to Worli meant moving schools, and I was now put in the G.K. Marg BMC English-Medium School. This school was a little better than the one in Colaba—we had regular exams and sports activities. Together with other children from poor communities, I was quickly labelled 'not a smart student'! Anyway, it was difficult to be smart in a school where questions and thinking were discouraged, and rote learning was praised. All BMC English-medium schools ended at Class 7, so there was no motivation for us to excel in academics, for there was no place to go after Class 7.

It was 1998, and I was 12 years old when I first heard about a free tuition class that had started in the Planetarium right next to our house. I had never been inside the building, or had tuitions. So, I was doubly excited. The next day I arrived at the entrance of the building at 8.30 a.m. and, following the other children who had shown up for class, I walked down a grand staircase to the basement. The interior design of the building had pictures of planets and many wall clocks—no two clocks had the same time! That was the first time I figured out that different places have different time zones, and I felt like an explorer who had discovered something completely new.

The classroom in the basement was cool—actually quite cold—with charts on the wall and colourful mats on the floor. Rajshree Didi greeted us with a big smile, '*Hum sab yahaan par padhenge aur bahut mazza karenge*' (We will all learn here, and have fun together). Sixty students were divided into groups of fifteen or twenty, and two or three teachers sat with each group. I was always in Level 3—the highest level. Anything and everything we learnt had meaning, and we learnt from anything and everything—integrated math and science, history and geography, English and marketing. We read Celine Dion's 'That's the Way It Is', the poet Kabir's dohas, acted out plays and sang songs. 'Superwoman' Rajshree Didi was the heart of our class. She could teach the most complicated concept in a simple and unique way. She held us together—teachers, volunteers and children.

Everything we did, reinforced a positive value. Didi's belief in the goodness of her students didn't shake—even for a second. And soon, no matter what our circumstances, we began to feel good about ourselves. She worked relentlessly to make sure that each of us turned out to be a good human being. Worli 1 (my Centre) became the showcase of Akanksha, and visitors came to see the rigour of our curriculum, and what a passionate teacher could bring into the classroom.

My first project at Akanksha was on 'The Difference between Education and Literacy'. It was a serious topic and as I researched in the Planetarium library and conducted surveys in the community, I felt mature and adult. Leadership qualities developed as we competed for responsibilities—Head Boy/Girl, Project Leader and Level Monitor. During career counselling sessions, parents and guest speakers were invited to give talks—a doctor, a driver, a writer, a gardener. To Didi, no work was too big, or too small. 'Do what your heart desires,' she would tell us, 'do what makes you happy, but do it with integrity and to the best of your ability.'

The teaching in the private school I was moved to after Class 7 was better than my BMC school, but the teachers were very strict, the fees was high and extra money was always needed for something or the other. My mother only earned around ₹2,000 per month, and I knew it was a struggle for her to manage expenses for the household and our education.

Akanksha focused on English and building foundation skills, more than on academic subjects. My English was good but other subjects were weak. I struggled through classes 8, 9 and 10. In my tuition class, punishments were harsh and when I did not memorize a lesson, I was hit on my knuckles with a wooden stick and had chili powder put on my tongue! Those were bad days, and I often thought of committing suicide. Now that I am the principal of a school, I have the authority to see that children are never humiliated or given corporal punishment.

After passing Class 10, I got admission into junior college. My college days were not typical of the average student. In the morning, I worked as a trainee in the HR Department at Akanksha; in afternoons, I attended college. In the evening I taught community kids; those who could afford it paid me a small fee, those who could not, I taught for free. It was always a packed day. There was no time to hang around in the canteen or participate in college fests. I was also timid and low on confidence, but I never felt that I was missing out on anything important.

I was not the usual college kid. Movies, clothes and jewellery did not interest me much and many free periods were spent with like-minded peers and professors, discussing philosophy and the value of education. There was no time to get mixed up in bad company. I did go out with friends, but not as much as other students. Being serious about my studies, I was eager to learn new things, honing one skill before moving on to a new one. In 2007, I was one of the first Akanksha students to graduate with a BCom degree.

After Class 12, I continued in the HR Department at Akanksha. My job included recruiting teachers from college campuses, keeping databases and filing. Upon completing college I worked full-time, taking on more responsibilities— giving presentations and conducting teacher training sessions. From the HR Department, I went on to Public Relations—learning about media and communication, designing, marketing and sales, and interacting with corporations and small business houses.

I worked with people who cared for me, and held me to high expectations. From Suparna Didi I learnt communication skills, Deepti Didi and Priya Didi taught me the rules for recruitment and Ruchi Didi sparked my creativity. These experiences gave me useful insights into myself. I need a sense of purpose and excitement to keep me involved in my work; I need to stay with something for a while before I know if it is right for me. An unexpected learning opportunity was a short-term assignment with Anjali Raina, at the Harvard Business School India Research Centre. Her daughter, Shveta, is a support and one of my closest friends.

At the end of the TFI Fellowship, another major choice had to be made—should I make my career in Commerce or teaching? Education became the default option to pursue. Having seen the progress I had made in my TFI classroom, I wanted to scale up to much more.

Gaurav Singh, a TFI alumnus, had set up the 321 Education Foundation with the goal of creating 100 schools for low-income kids. In 2012, I joined 321 as one of the founding members and taught kindergarten at the Mahatma Jyotiba Phule Market (MPS) English-Medium School—a public-private partnership (PPP) with the municipality. We organized teacher training courses and shared best teaching practices within the larger education system. Two beacon phrases—'Excellence is a habit' and 'Grace under pressure'—guided the teachers.

321 became my life, and the relationships I formed there are most precious to me. The four years I worked with Gaurav gave me valuable insights into education and life. I am very grateful to him.

In my third year at 321, I was appointed school principal, and the holistic education I had experienced at Akanksha, became the path for our school. Unfortunately, the public-private partnership policy between the municipality and 321 was not implemented as envisioned, and did not align with our model or mission. The two main issues were the delays in getting space and permissions, and the refusal and timings of financial reimbursements. In May 2016, 321 handed over the management of the school to the Akanksha Foundation. It was an extremely hard and emotional decision to take, but we believe it was the right one.

Three organizations have shaped me: Akanksha built my foundation and gave me the first opportunities; TFI, the courage and confidence to become a leader; and at 321, I found the space and encouragement to do what I do best—be a teacher.

Many special people have been and remain a part of my life—Rajshree Didi, my first and dearest teacher at Akanksha, with whom I can share anything, ask any question and know I will get an honest answer. Since I was a child, Shaheen Didi has been my inspiration, and I have watched her do even the smallest thing with the greatest love. Anu Didi, a corporate leader, simple and kind, taught me to respect everyone, no matter who they are.

But it is my mother's love and support that has made everything possible. Mummy worked long hours as a cleaner in the Navy School, but she never burdened me with housework, insisting I spend all my time on studies. She used to leave the house before the sun was out, but always had time to comb my hair neatly for school. She is open-minded and trusts my decisions. I can stay out late at night and have the freedom to dress the way I want—whether in jeans or a sleeveless blouse. Our relationship has developed into one that I value greatly.

Family is important to me. Nilesh, my older brother, dropped out of school in Class 5, but has finally found work in the hotel industry. He is married, has one child and is well-settled. Shailesh and I are very close. He is the middle one, and, unable to cope with studies, left school in Class 8. Later, things worked out for him and he is now an office boy in a finance company.

In May 2016, I proudly represented Akanksha at the 25th Anniversary Gala in New York. I spoke from the heart and told my story. After I finished speaking, many guests came up, wanting to sponsor both my school and me. The overwhelming response at the Gala revealed that people everywhere believe that every child has a right to an excellent education. One of the highlights of the evening was hearing Salman, another Akanksha alumnus, talk about his experiences. I learnt an important lesson from him that night—be easy on yourself and enjoy the little things, no matter what the circumstances.

I live in two very separate worlds—inside and outside the community. My preference is not to live in Mariamma, and sometime back, I rented out our flat to the builder, and took a nice flat in a safe area. I liked it, but it did not work out for the rest of the family. They missed community life, and mother was frightened that if we stayed away too long, the builder would not return our flat. So after four years we returned to Mariamma, which now, thankfully, has the basic facilities of water and indoor toilets. Most importantly—my mother likes it here.

I am glad I was born where I was. It gave me the drive to push for something better, the appreciation for what I got, and the opportunity to meet people I would never have met. I am glad I was born where I was. It has made me who I am today.

∞

*'My most joyous moment was when I got a part-time job after
Class 12 and took on the family responsibility, so that my
mother no longer had to go out to work.'*

ASHISH KOLI | AKANKSHA | 2000 TO 2013
BA final year, Fine Arts, Abhinav Kala Mahavidyalay, Pashan, near Pune
Date of Birth: 13 April 1994

THE REBEL ARTIST

I love to draw pictures. Ever since I was a child, I have been drawing anything that came to my mind—fruits, birds, animals, and later, even cartoons. Today, I am in the final year of my graduate diploma at the College of Fine Arts in Pune. And I still love to draw.

Creative activities, in one form or another, have always attracted me. My interest in photography was sparked in 2014, when I worked at Cannon Inc for two years, and this experience has given me a strong desire to go around the world with a camera in my hand—New York, Paris, Dubai...

Taking photographs of nature, especially attracts me—birds and animals in their natural habitat, the patterned wings and bodies of insects, and the many varieties of flowers, each one different from the other. I edit my photos on Photoshop and CorelDRAW, and would like to learn macro-photography—enlarging landscapes and portraits to give the viewer a feel of the real thing. Art and photography combine well and I see how effective they are in advertisements and 3D movies.

I developed my drawing and painting skills under Sonya Didi's guidance in the art class at the Akanksha Centre. Learning the different techniques, I had the opportunity to exhibit a painting in the Madhubani Painting Exhibition organized by Tech Mahindra, and paint a mural in the children's ward at

Sassoon Hospital, which I hope the children are still enjoying. Experimenting further, I started painting on different objects, and covered a large box with a jungle theme—animals, birds and rivers. One day, a college friend, Durgesh Naik, drew tattoos on my hand and I got interested in tattoo art. Now I make good money as a tattoo artist. All types of art interests me.

Life is about connections. Akanksha connected me to art, and my father connected me to Akanksha. One evening, I was playing in the street with my gang of boys when two unknown women came up to us and asked, 'Can we play with you guys?' Giving back a rude reply—I can't remember what—we ran away. The women went to Papa's shop and when he heard that they had come to enrol children for a study centre they were starting, he saw a good learning opportunity for my sister, Asha, and me. I did not think it was a good idea at all—because I was already in a Marathi school and did not want to go to another class!

But I was afraid of Papa and his wishes had to be obeyed. At dinner that same day, I heard details about this new class. It was located at Matoshri Ashram, and we would be picked up from home and dropped back to the community. It was a morning class and the subjects being taught included English and mathematics. 'Best of all,' said Papa, 'it is for free.' My father convinced the other parents that it was a good programme, and when the manager of Matoshri Ashram guaranteed that the project was okay, many families agreed to send their children to the Centre.

I knew that this new arrangement was going to upset my routine. For when we were not at school, my friends and I were part of a street gang—teasing strangers and picking up fights on the street. To tell the truth, I was sort of the leader—pushing my friends to make trouble in the community. When we were not causing damage we played our favourite game, 'Chini-OK'. The kid in the centre of a circle called aloud 'Chini' and the players around chanted OK, OK, OK... The player in the centre threw a stick over his shoulder to those behind him. If the stick was not caught by one of the boys in the circle, the person in the centre had to get to the fallen stick in exactly five steps, or he was declared out! It was not a very clever game but we had such fun playing it.

When I went to Akanksha, I took my street language and behaviour with me, but soon the good examples set by the older children changed my way of thinking. My language became acceptable, my behaviour improved; I got involved in studies and new activities at the Centre. In fact, I loved going to class so much that every year I received a certificate for above 85 per cent attendance!

My success at the Centre flowed over to my Marathi school, and the teachers noticed my progress—I got the highest marks in English and mathematics, and won speech and essay-writing competitions. In school, students teased me when I spoke in English, but soon, everyone wanted to speak English the way I did—I can't explain how good that felt!

My interests widened and I participated in sports (especially football), cultural activities and drama. My father says that Akanksha made a huge positive change in my personality and he was right. Gone was the abusive, disruptive Ashish! I liked this new me!

When I click on my Akanksha memories, I see 'Matoshri'—an old-age home on the bank of the Mutha River. It was established by the NGO, Raja Shri Shivrai Pratishthan. As part of Akanksha's Social Service activities, we celebrated Raksha Bandhan with the elderly uncles and aunties at the home. Singing songs for them and tying the coloured bands on their wrists, I felt content—happy.

A field trip to the Aga Khan Palace, where Gandhiji had been imprisoned, was better than a history lesson, and visits to Frame Box, an animation training institute, and Patni Computers gave me a look into the world of information technology. I also worked as an intern in the administrative department of TFI. Each experience widened my mind and took me physically and mentally beyond the limits of my community, Nava Sahyadri. There were career guidance talks and preparation for interviews and internships. Scholarships were also available for those who deserved them.

I have grown up in Nava Sahyadri in Karvenagar, Pune, with caring and supportive families around me—the Fawades, Pols, Kadams, Bokefodes and Padavals. Together, we became one enormous family. There were always friends to play with and adults to solve our problems. But the physical conditions in the community were terrible—when I was a child, there were no toilets in the house, and we had to go outside, crouching in corners and behind walls. There was also no water line in our area, and we walked 10 kms to fetch water! After some years we complained to Medha Kulkarni, the Nagarsevak, and toilets were built and water pipelines installed in each house. I cannot imagine how we lived with such bad facilities for so many years. Tolerance is not always a good quality to have!

Papa is a simple man. He used to repair punctures in bicycles, motorbikes, trucks and cars; and he also ran a shop in front of our house, selling milk, egg, curds and ice cream. In the last four years, his health has not been good and he now works as an office boy in Anshuman Tech Pvt Ltd.

Mummy is a housewife, and she was the one who taught me the difference between right and wrong and how to conduct myself in difficult situations. Papa was strict, Mummy was soft. Religion was a big part of their daily life and became a part of mine too. As children, we watched our parents doing the pooja and arti in religious ceremonies, and went to our village for the annual yatra (pilgrimage). In the last few years, my parents have become more open-minded, and now we celebrate many religious festivals.

When I was a child, my day began early. After freshening up and getting dressed, I would be at the shop by 7 a.m. to help Papa. The Akanksha class was from 8.30 a.m. to 11 a.m. and my Marathi school, Dnyanda Prashala, was from noon until 6 p.m. As soon as I got home, my parents saw that I completed my homework, after which I was free to roam the streets with friends until 9 p.m.

Through school and college, football has been a serious hobby, and for eight years I played at the Parshuramiyan Club with the coach, Ameya Sir. Now I teach football at three Akanksha centres and at my Club. Like most young Indian men, I love cricket, and on 13 April 2010, my sixteenth birthday, I got the best birthday present ever—the opportunity to watch an IPL match. It was also special because my best friend, Kiran More, was with me, and we were in a group with Nita Ambani, one of Akanksha's sponsors.

All parents want job security for their children, and after finishing school in Class 10, Papa persuaded me to take Commerce (Arts was considered too easy and Science too difficult). I agreed to try it out even though my heart was really in the Arts. However, when I failed in junior college, Papa allowed me to transfer to visual arts and I did well in the basic Foundation Diploma. I went on to study commercial art in the College for Fine Arts, but was totally unaware that the college was not officially certified. After three years of hard study, and paying the fees, we were shocked to read in the newspapers that our college was illegal! There was a big protest among parents, and the principal promised to get us admission into a certified college—but he took no action.

Disappointed and angry that three years of our study and fees had been wasted, the students took control of the situation. We went to Mumbai to meet Mr Tikhe, chairman of the J.J. School of Art (Kala Sanchanalay), who assured us that we would be admitted into other certified colleges as final-year students. For fifteen days we commuted daily between Pune and Mumbai, trying to solve the problem, but the result was not what we had expected. Most students did get into other art colleges, but had to repeat the three years they had already completed. What a waste of time and money! I refused to repeat the three years of college that I had already passed, and applied to twenty or thirty colleges until I finally got admission in the fourth year at Abhinav Kala Mahavidyalaya at Pashan, near Pune. The best thing about this college is that the landscape around is green and fresh, and everything looks new and hopeful.

I have a short list of people who have inspired me: my mentor, Abhijeet Bhaiya; the founders of the NAAN Foundation, Nana Patekar, Makarand Anaspure and Sayaji Shinde, who support the families of farmers who committed suicide and contribute to the education and marriages of their children; Salman Khan and Sachin Tendulkar, well-known public figures, who fund the education of kids from low-income families.

But the first and best inspiration has come from my home. Papa's schooling ended in Class 5, and though Mummy can read and write a little bit, she never went to school. But they both made sure that their children got a good education. Asha, my sister, also an Akanksha alumnus, is a BCom graduate completing her MBA in Human Resources and working in the administration office of Era Hydro Biotech Energy Ltd. All their lives, my parents lived in a very small space, and even the basic necessities were not available to them. Asha and I are working to give them an easier, better life.

In 2017, I will graduate in Fine Arts but would prefer to make a career in photography. Perhaps, the best option would be to combine photography, graphic design and illustration. A more immediate goal is to land a job at 'Affinity' as a Graphic and Web Designer. Once I am settled at work, like Sonya Didi, I will share my love for art and photography with children who didn't have the opportunities that I did.

Photography, design, drawing, football and tattooing—I see them all as part of my future. I see our family living in our own lavish home. I see myself trying to be a good son and good brother, later, a good husband, good father, and always a good human being.

❦

'In 2017, I will graduate in Fine Arts but would prefer to make
a career in photography. Perhaps the best option would be to
combine photography, graphic design and illustration.'

Ashish was a good human being. Sadly, the landscape around his college that he described as green and fresh, new and hopeful did not predict his future. He had a tragic death on 13 December 2016. He was 22 years old.

SAMEER SHEIKH | AKANKSHA | 1995 TO 2005
BCom
Police Constable, Detective Branch, Shivaji Nagar Police Station
Date of Birth: 17 September 1991

THE ROAD TO THE POLICE ACADEMY

A quick temper and a bad habit of getting into fights always got me into trouble. One day, sitting with friends outside my home, we saw a woman run out of her house. Her husband had torn off her clothes in a fit of anger and trying to protect herself from him, she had rushed out naked. Seeing the terrified look on her face, I ran to help her, but the husband came after me and stabbed me with a knife—I still have the scar. I was furious, and grabbing a bamboo stick that was lying around, I broke the man's leg!

Of course I was taken to the police station. The wife must have been so frightened of her husband that she told the police that I had started the fight! My Akanksha didis and bhaiyas and my friends pleaded with the police not to register a complaint against me. Luckily, I was let off. I met that same woman seven years later; she apologized to me for her false statement to the police and thanked me for trying to protect her from her husband! Would I rush to save an abused woman today? I think I would—but I would not break her husband's leg!

Ammi and Abba were too busy to know what was happening in the lives of their five daughters and two sons. Every morning at 7 a.m. my mother took the train to Lonavala, 72 kms from Pune. From an area allotted to her, she collected scrap materials that she sold to bangar-wallahs. Abba, an electrician, supplied lights for wedding mandaps (pavilions) and interiors. Whatever money he got from his work, he spent on alcohol, and when he needed more, he took Ammi's earnings. Abba was too drunk to worry about his children; Ammi, that sweet lady, was busy working and running the house.

My parents never knew which class we were studying in, where we were, or what we were doing. All my sisters remained illiterate and were later married off. We seven siblings controlled our own lives, adjusting ourselves to different situations. Being the youngest, I was especially scared of both Ammi and Abba, and had to plan well in advance if I needed to ask them for money or anything else.

At Akanksha, I found the attention and care I did not get at home. My friend, Vishal, who is a great guy and a great dancer, invited me to a Christmas party at his Akanksha Centre, a class, he said, where they read English poems and ate cake. It sounded fun and like a thief I slunk in through a back door. It was a good party, and after a month I went back on my own, and followed the other children into a classroom. Maushi, who was a mother of one of the children and assisted the teacher, introduced me to Sumitra Didi and Ketki Didi, *'Yeh ladka pehlay aya tha centre ko'* (this boy has come to the Centre earlier). Without asking who I was or why I had come, the teachers welcomed me to the class, and from that day on I became an Akanksha student. I was 10 years old.

For me, the highlight of the Centre's curriculum was sports, and I used to wait eagerly for Saturday and Sunday, when we had athletics and sports activities. On my first annual sports day, thirty-two Akanksha centres in Pune came together and every student had to take part in at least one event. I won gold medals in long jump, shot put and the 100-m race! Subhash Bhaiya, our sports teacher, came up to congratulate me, and that was when I first thought of a career in sports.

Away from the sports field, I had problems. Academics did not interest me, in fact, Santosh Bhaiya, a social worker, often had to drag me out of my home and into the class. At the Centre, I fought with other students and had arguments with teachers and volunteers. Once I was suspended from class for six months because I had a big fight with my best friend. My name was dropped from the sports class, and I was not permitted to compete on Sports Day. This was a terrible punishment, for I loved sports and was excellent at it. There were other consequences—I did not get to play in an important district-level cricket match; or attend the IPL match between Mumbai and the Royal Challengers, missing the opportunity to meet Sachin Tendulkar, the superstar of Indian cricket.

At the Centre, my bad marks, behaviour and attitude forced Reeves Bhaiya to call my mother to the office. Ammi was so ashamed that she cried right there—in Bhaiya's office. Seeing this, I was very upset, and from that day I made a big effort to change my lifestyle. Living in Patil Estate, Pune, this was not easy. The community was a hub of illegal activities—ganja and charas were freely traded, gang violence was common, petty smugglers were everywhere and illicit liquor flowed in the houses and dirty lanes. Without the support of people like Kanchan Didi, and my bhaiyas, Santosh and Reeves, I could have never made it.

In my regular PMC school, things were even worse. I bunked school, was bored in class and my marks were terrible. My parents had no idea of my situation in school. When I was disqualified from appearing for the final boards because of my irregular attendance, I really panicked. Santosh Bhaiya begged the school to give me another chance and they agreed. I was given a strict warning, 'Sameer, without studying, nothing will happen in your life. You will always live in Patil Estate and be in the same situation as your parents.' I promised Bhaiya that I would pass the examination, filled in the forms and started studying—but still played cricket on weekends! The exam was in a month's time—maybe it was already too late to make up what I had missed? The exam papers were tough, but with luck, I passed, though my marks were not good.

The next challenge was to decide what I should do after Class 10. Parag Chawat, my mentor at Akanksha, gave me the best advice, 'Sameer, do what you are interested in.' We met every Saturday and discussed the week's programme and career possibilities. With his encouragement, I applied and got admission in a two-year government diploma course in electronics, after which I would be eligible to go to a college of my choice.

At home, the family was struggling to meet expenses and again I followed Bhaiya's advice to work and study at the same time. I was a security guard from 9 p.m. to 8 a.m., went to college in the afternoon, and from 6 p.m. to 8 p.m. studied at the Centre. I followed this schedule for two years and passed my final exams with good scores! Students must leave Akanksha after Class 10. It had been an amazing eight years. From Reeves Bhaiya, Santosh Bhaiya and Kanchan Didi I learnt to respect people, speak correctly, live with good values, and even eat properly. I miss those days.

After completing the diploma course, I got admission to

Tikaram Jagganath College, Pune University, for a BCom degree. Accounting and Costing were tough subjects and in the first term I failed in Accounting—with a score of just 1 out of 80! Fortunately, Mansi Didi and Shweta Didi found Chandrashekar Bhaiya—a great teacher. I gave up the security job, and working more reasonable hours, I became an administrative assistant at Akanksha and ran sports classes for children at the same Centre where I had been a student. It was the perfect job for me—I knew exactly the sports activities the kids needed and would enjoy.

In my second year at college, I played national-level rugby for the Pune team. At one of the rugby practices, I met a friend from the Police Academy, and that got me thinking about a career in the Police Force—it would be a satisfying and respectful profession. But many admissions to the Force had caste reservations; since I belonged to an open caste, I was not eligible for them.

In the first year, I gave the exams from the Pune rural quota. We were required to pass the physical examination and a written paper, both very tough. I failed to make it to the merit list, scoring 173 out of 200—the cut-off mark was 175. This was my bad luck! In 2014, after completing my BCom, I reapplied to the Police Force from the Pune city area, and topped the final merit list. I had reached my first goal.

In the Maharashtra Police Bharti exam 2014, I scored 190 out of 200—definitely the biggest achievement of my life. When I reported to the police station, a senior officer looked at the home address on my papers and mocked me, '*Aap abhi police hue ho, yahan Patil Estate wali harkat nahi karna*' (Now that you have become a policeman, don't follow Patil Estate's practices here). I felt humiliated, but quickly answered back, '*Aap ko pata hai is bharti me jo pehla ladka aya hai, Patil Estate mein rehta hai* ' (do you know that the boy who stood first in this batch lives in Patil Estate). It was the officer's turn to feel ashamed—he turned and quickly walked away without saying a word!

Everyone in the community came to congratulate me. But one person was not there—my father. He had died six months earlier and would never see his son in a police uniform. I miss my father—now there is no one whom I can call Abba.

I take my job very seriously. The police department has a duty to solve problems—an important role to play everywhere in the world. Can you imagine what would happen if the entire Pune police force decided to go on leave at the same time? There would be chaos!

I started by working in the local crime department, where people register complaints. Now I am a police constable in the detective branch of Shivaji Nagar Police Station. We are the first points of contact for citizens when they want to report a crime. Once a crime is reported, we investigate and solve the case. When a criminal escapes from prison, it is our responsibility to nab the criminal. While working on a case we do not wear uniforms; we blend in with the crowd, not attracting attention. I am very aware that I carry a big responsibility.

I met Saleha when we were both training on the Police Sports grounds. We got married in 2016. It was a love marriage, and her Rajput family objected because I come from a different caste. Now they have slowly come around to accepting me. Saleha is also in the police force—her present job is to recruit and train policewomen, but she is ambitious and hardworking and would like to hold a police inspector's post. I hope she does—very soon.

We have moved from Patil Estate to police quarters—our standard of living has improved and my family is respected in the community. Ammi, who is like God to me, lives happily with us, and no longer has to go out to work. Saleha and I readily compromise our own wishes to keep the family happy, for their happiness is important to us. My elder brother is an electrician and owns an autorickshaw; I am saving to buy him a house. The birth of our son, Arshad, on 12 November 2016, was the greatest joy of all. My life is now complete.

When I visit my old home in Patil Estate (especially in my uniform), the community kids see me as a role model. Soon I am going to start Police Bharti (admission) classes for young men and women, giving guidance on how to qualify for the police force. They will learn what I did—unless you achieve something, no one is going to respect you.

My wife encourages me to study for the inter-departmental examinations. Hopefully, I will keep rising—to the level of Police Sub-inspector, Joint Commissioner and then Additional Commissioner of Police. To be an effective leader, I have to develop patience, speaking skills, take the lead in solving problems and make decisions with maturity. Playing sports has taught me a useful lesson—in life, as in rugby and football, what is more important than winning or losing, is how you face defeat and how quickly you get back into the game.

Santosh Bhaiya has guided me for so many years and I must end this story with him. He taught me to control my temper, pushed me to study, showed me my potential, and always turned up when I was in trouble. Bhaiya, I hope you think it was worth all that effort!

∽

'Playing sports has taught me a useful lesson—in life,
as in rugby and football, what is more important than winning
or losing, is how you face defeat and how quickly you get back
into the game.'

NAHEEDA ANSARI | AKANKSHA | 1996 TO 2003
BA, Sociology and Education (NIOS)
Senior KG teacher, Abhyudaya Nagar School, Mumbai
Date of Birth: 22 October 1983

TEACHING WITH PASSION

It was my bua (aunt) who decided that it was time for my two older sisters, aged 13 and 16, to be pulled out of school and get married. Not wanting to go against her wishes, Mummy and Daddy agreed with her. Both my sisters were first-rankers— dedicated to their studies and with aspirations to succeed in life. But their happiness was short-lived. Even if they had protested against an early marriage, they knew no one would listen to them, for the pressure from the relatives and the community would decide their future. I knew that I was next in line.

My parents were uneducated and did not give importance to education. But being in an Akanksha Centre, I was highly motivated to continue studying, and there was no way that I would leave and be married off!

Rajshree Didi, my guiding light, came to our house several times to convince my parents that I should finish my studies before marriage. Once Didi had started the momentum, I had the will to continue the fight! It was my journey and I knew I must take the initiative and speak up for myself. Mummy and Daddy, following Didi's advice, allowed me to remain at the Centre. I look back and realize what a life-altering decision my parents and I took those many years ago. Today, I am smiling.

But my journey did not begin smoothly. I found English particularly tough. Perhaps it was because I studied in different mediums, and in so many schools. Until Class 4, I had been in an Urdu school in the village, and then for two to three years I did not go to school at all. My next shift was to the English-medium Anjuman Islam School, where I struggled for two years and then for a year I was put in a BMC school. The didis, thinking that my progress was fine, moved me to the private J.J. High School. When I failed in Class 7, I was removed from the school. These changes confused me; school became a nightmare and I gave up. Mummy had a small grocery shop and I went to help her with it. In short, my early experiences made me hate school—staying at home was much more fun.

My younger siblings were part of the Akanksha Centre at St Xavier's College. Often, I took my brother to the Centre and hid behind a tree or a door to watch the activities in his class. I did not know that while I was watching the children, someone was watching me! One day, a lady came up to me and asked if I wanted to join the Centre—I answered at once—yes! And this is where my story really began.

For seven years I was at Akanksha—two and a half hours every day. After I graduated from the Centre at 18, I was offered a post in a BMC/Akanksha school, as an Assistant Art Teacher. The students in BMC schools deserve a much better quality of education than they are given. This was a chance for me to try and bring in some improvements.

Sriram Bhaiya was the manager of the school, and since we both had the same bus route, we went home together, shared stories, built trust, and developed a close relationship. He persuaded me to give the Class 10 exam through NIOS. I failed in my first attempt, but was now motivated enough to not give up, and tried again and passed Class 10 and later Class 12.

I went on studying by distance education and graduated with a BA double major in Sociology and Education. It had taken a long time, but with Bhaiya's encouragement pushing me on, I did it. However, my real schooling was at the Centre, for what I learnt there has become a part of my daily life.

The two programmes that groomed me and gave me courage were the SLP and the three-year Akanksha Teacher Fellowship. I saw the impact of SLP's influence on me on the day when I witnessed a road accident, near the Doordarshan TV building in Mumbai. Nobody in the crowd that was gathered around the accident was helping the injured couple. I took the initiative— went with the couple to the hospital, reported the accident to the police station, completed the lengthy police procedures and got home late in the night. The next morning, I went back to the hospital, with nariyal pani (coconut water) and biscuits. It was the first time I had gone out of my way to help strangers.

The SLP also inspired me and nine friends to start Pragati, an NGO, to cheer up and support kids in hospitals. Children recover faster when they are happy, and parents are less tense when they see their children smiling. Our job is to occupy the children with activities and be there for the mums and dads.

The Teacher Fellowship I received at Akanksha boosted my interest in teaching. It gave me a chance to work with children and I made sure that my students didn't go through the same bad school experiences that I did. Fear was a big part of my school life—I was scared to speak in class, always frightened of what the teacher would say or do if I did not understand something, or if I needed an explanation. If my head was not covered with a scarf or I forgot to wear a salwar under my skirt, I was beaten with a thick stick. Today, as a teacher, I encourage students to come to me if they are confused, immediately giving them all my attention.

I am a Senior KG teacher in the Abhyudaya Nagar School run by Akanksha. In ten years of teaching, I have learnt a lot, especially from Rajshree Didi—she showed me how to stand up for what I believe in, and made me see that every child has a unique potential, whether he or she does well or not. Learning must be fun, for boring lessons make dull and morose children. In my class, I make sure that no child is left behind.

I have a lovely story on the importance of teachers being alert and aware in the classroom. One of my students always insisted that I eat something from his tiffin—two chips, a biscuit— any snack he brought to class. One day, he gave me a packet that was all wrapped up, and without asking him what it was, I told him to put it back in his bag. When his mother came to pick him up, she was surprised to see the packet still in the bag. She explained that when the boy was sick, the doctor had given him almonds and dates to make him strong. The child, thinking that I looked thin and weak, had brought some nuts to make me well, and I had not even taken the trouble to ask the boy why he wanted to give me the packet!

Circle Time at Akanksha was a favourite activity and my kids love it too. We sit in a circle, each child sharing something with the group. It is a platform for students to express their emotions and views—who they love most and why, what things they don't like to do, what makes them happy or sad. Listening to each other, children become more sympathetic to the other children in class.

It is absolutely essential for teachers to connect with parents and win their trust. I do this in different ways—talking to mothers when they come to pick up their kids, home visits, and parent-teacher meetings where mothers are given practical advice on how to manage eating habits, and learning and behavioural problems.

Usually, parents spend the most time with their children and they have the most influence on them. If a mother understands the importance of education, the child will value their school. Physical punishments by parents is a sensitive issue and must be handled carefully. If I notice that a child has been beaten, I never accuse the parent straightaway, for it is difficult to judge a parent's reaction. Trust between teacher and parent is the only way to change things and make them better.

Children will perform well when they feel physically and emotionally safe. Teachers do get tired and frustrated, but they must never, never hit a student. My kids learn without me ever raising a hand on them.

It is not easy for children to express their problems and teachers must analyse a situation before responding to it. A boy in my class kept touching and taking out his penis. He said it was itching, and continued the same behaviour. The mother's first reaction when I told her about it, was to beat him; but working together and without punishment, he was able to stop this habit.

Rajshree Didi has influenced me more than anyone else. She always had time to listen to me, and today I tell parents, 'Pay attention to what your child says, sit and listen to what is happening in school.' Simple questions—How do you feel today? Who is your film hero? What was the best thing you did in school?—make children feel important.

Getting students to think is a challenge. Didi would listen

to my question and turn it back to me, 'Naheeda, what do you think is the solution? Think and make a decision.' I ask my children to find their own solutions!

More than anything, I want my students to be good human beings. Through games and activities, I try and develop good values, and hope that when facing a conflict they will figure out for themselves what is the right thing to do.

It is not enough for individuals and some schools to make the necessary changes, the Indian government's school system needs reform. Sometimes I sit and think of the improvements I would make.

The quickest way to bring about change is to invest in high-quality training of teachers, for it is the teachers who will shape our country. We must bring in passionate teachers, dedicated to their work—teachers who are open-minded and respect every religion. To develop such leaders, promotions must be given based on performance and not on caste or tribe reservations. Teachers should not be given administrative jobs and government duties. These cut into preparation and teaching time. Efficient time management will give teachers and students more learning and play time.

The pressure of exams, and rote learning of subjects, is an unnecessary burden on students and needs to be examined. Exams should be application-based, as the purpose of exams is to test knowledge together with the understanding of the content. Teachers who encourage children to learn, and not mechanically follow and complete the given syllabus, will produce thinking students.

Government schools must be well-maintained. I really believe that children have a right to a good education in a nice building—a school they can be proud of.

I have got carried away by my passion for teaching, and how children can learn and be happy in school, and have left little space to write about my family, who are very important to me. We live in a small house, never complaining about our situation and thankful to Allah for giving us what we have. There will come a time when I can buy a bigger house—one in which the whole family can live and celebrate the festival of Eid together.

While we were growing up, my parents imposed many restrictions on us, but I truly value Mummy and Daddy today. If they had not educated me, I would have been a mother of three or four children by now and missed out on all the experiences I have had.

My father was a BMC employee, a motor-loader—now he is retired. Mummy was very strict, and we were not allowed to make friends or bring anyone home, because they would be a bad influence on us. We were beaten a lot, sometimes even a bone would get broken! Nobody could stop Daddy when he wanted to do something, and neighbours stopped helping us, because when he got violent they were scared that he would beat them up too!

Mummy used to go out to sell vegetables, and a lot of the housework responsibility was on our shoulders—washing bartans (utensils), taking care of the younger siblings, doing the jharoo (sweeping) and other things in the house. So we learnt to adjust and work hard early in life—as early as the age of 5.

My parents are happy that I am educated and financially independent, and have now given me the freedom to choose a life partner on my own. Either love or arranged, I must get to know my husband well before marriage. He must be someone who understands me—my companion for life. Soon I hope to get married, and when I do, I will be a good mother to my kids, supporting them in whatever they want to do, and teaching them to be caring citizens.

My goal is to be a school principal, where I will have the authority to put into practice some of the things I believe in. At some stage, together with Sangeeta, Neeta and Anjali, all Akanksha alumni, I will open a kindergarten—a cheerful, non-restricting, no-pressure school that does not punish children when their alphabet and number writing goes out of the red and blue lines of their copy book!

As a child, I was as stubborn, badly behaved and scared of failure as many children are today. Now I speak up with confidence for what I believe in. This is my life, and I need to live it the way I want. One day my students will say just that.

∽

'It is not enough for individuals and some schools to make the necessary changes, the Indian government's school system needs reform. The quickest way to bring about change is to invest in high-quality training of teachers, for it is the teachers who will shape our country.'

POOJA WAGH | AKANKSHA | 2002 TO 2012
BCom, Marathwada Mitra Mandal's College of Commerce
Chartered Accountant
Date of Birth: 4 September 1992

SUCCESS AT A PRICE

Papa was so heartbroken when my eldest sister failed her Class 10 exam that he pulled all five of us out of school. Madhura was in a private school, the rest of us studied in a government institution. After her failure, none of us were allowed to complete our education.

My sisters started working to support the family, and ultimately all got married—Madhura, at the early age of 17. Today, one of my brothers works with a relative while the other is an autorickshaw driver.

Aajoba, my grandfather, passed away when father was about 8 years old, and Papa had to leave school to take care of my grandmother and uncles. He used to walk from the village to sell vegetables in the city—many kilometres away. That is how he managed to support his large family.

My grandmother had health issues, and so grandfather also had to do the household tasks—cooking, cleaning, washing, etc. Even after Papa got married, he had big responsibilities, for apart from his seven children, he took care of a cousin whose father had died.

We understood his situation and compromised, sacrificing our own wishes because we knew he was doing the best he could for us. Papa's difficult childhood must have influenced his own beliefs, for he had strict principles and very definite ideas. One of them was his bias against girls, and only after having five daughters was his desire fulfilled—he had two sons.

It is easier to go against the world than to stay in the same house and oppose one's parents. My father was the decision-maker of the family and the consequences were horrible if anyone went against his wishes. Aai, my mother, wanted us to study further but my father did not. I fought against his decision to stop my studies and he finally said I could go back to school—only, if I sponsored my own education. I started working when I was in Class 8.

We lived in a 1 BHK house, and though small, the size was not an issue—we fitted our regular schedule into the space we had. The people in our community were generally uneducated, selfish, narrow-minded—and being around them was demotivating. On the other hand, some neighbours were very helpful, and there was no religious discrimination in the community.

I went to the Hutatma Shirshkumar School, where we just studied what was needed to clear exams. School knowledge, it appeared, was only required to get a degree. My real education began when I joined the Akanksha Wakdewadi Centre. In the beginning, Aai was not ready to send me to the Centre. She had heard that kids could be kidnapped from there, and when she saw Mrs Anu Aga, a trustee, who looked like a foreigner, Aai became very suspicious!

For a long time, I went to class without informing my mother, and only later when she was convinced that Anu Didi was not a foreigner and Akanksha was a proper class, did she permit me to attend it.

Akanksha opened in Pune in 2002 and I was enrolled in

one of the very first batches. The office and the Centre were in the same bungalow, with separate classrooms for different learning levels. Every day after school, I spent two and a half hours at the Centre. We were a crazy group of friends and drove away each and every teacher—until Karishma Didi came. Our classroom was in the kitchen, and every time Didi went to supervise another level, the class stopped work and danced around—when she returned we pretended to be studying! We disrupted lessons with silly jokes and non-stop laughter that brought Didi to tears, but she still loved us.

After Karishma Didi, there was a line of didis and bhaiyas who tried to control us and then Reeves Bhaiya arrived—a tough teacher. His classes went on until 10 p.m.; he made sure we had the maximum possible time to learn. It was much later that we realized that Bhaiya's strictness was for our own good. We learnt much more than what was in the curriculum—we understood the meaning of women's empowerment, social leadership and career building. Bhaiya taught me until I graduated, and I remember that on the last day, all of us—students, teachers and volunteers—cried as we said our goodbyes. I wanted to stay in the Centre for a lifetime. I am still in touch with Bhaiya and keep him updated on the happenings in my life. In spite of my naughtiness and defiance, my childhood at Akanksha was full of love, activities and opportunities. It provided me a platform to represent myself to the world.

On the day I got my Class 10 results, Papa was so anxious to know my marks that he took time off from the juice centre that he runs. When he heard that I ranked first in my division, his eyes lit with happiness. Since then, whenever I clear any exam, he distributes at least five kilos of sweets!

After my first academic success, Papa's attitude to education changed and he respected my determination to continue my studies. When I went for admission to the Marathwada Mitra Mandal's College of Commerce, he stood in the queue along with me and accompanied me to college for one whole week, until I was familiar with the new location. He was now ready to finance my college education but I insisted on being independent and worked in my sister's catering business—managing and scheduling customers' orders and earning ₹50 per order.

However, to fully support my education, I needed more funds, and I joined Akanksha as a trainee in the HR Department. It was a hectic schedule—morning college, afternoons in HR training to improve my communication and presentation skills with Mansi Didi (hats off to you Didi, for your commitment and dedication to your work), and in the evenings there were accounting classes. Chandrasekharan Bhaiya encouraged me to take up CA as a career. I did not think it was my cup of tea or that I would succeed, but Bhaiya pushed me to sit for the intermediate exam—and surprisingly I passed at the very first attempt. I have a special bonding with Mansi Didi and Chandrasekharan Bhaiya, and whenever I got tense before a CA exam, I used to talk to them and feel relaxed. They are equivalent to my parents and I feel lucky to have them in my life.

The challenges in the career I have chosen excite me. Economies change, and as they do, I update my knowledge and learn new things. CA is a tough course, but I am interested in accounts and taxation, and this is the best platform to learn and practise these subjects. It is also a profession that commands respect and can definitely open up many opportunities.

As I worked for the final CA exam, my schedule did not

get easier. The day started with coaching classes at 4 a.m., after which I did my articleship, followed by more coaching, and studying in the Ahilya Library until night. I never got enough sleep. There were no Pune Municipal Transport (PMT) buses early morning or late at night, and my back ached carrying around heavy books. Since the location where we stay is not very safe, and there are no street lights to light up the dark roads, my mother would accompany me every morning up to Shivaji Nagar.

After a year, I developed eye problems and had two operations. It became difficult for me to walk alone for a long distance, and a special friend of mine who worked in the firm where I was doing my articleship, took me to my classes. He also taught me to ride a bike, and now that I own one, there are no transport problems. This same friend has contributed to my success in many ways—sometime soon I hope to be able to help him.

The IPCC was the first big CA exam. Despite studying fifteen hours a day, I was so nervous that even before I started writing the first paper, I broke three pens! Then I thought of Mansi Didi and Chandrasekharan Bhaiya, who had done so much to help me. I had to succeed as much for them as for myself—I picked up the broken pen and started writing. I did well in the intermediate exam and was now properly convinced that I was in the right field.

My success came at a high cost. A few days before my IPCC exam my grandfather died, and giving priority to my exam, I did not even attend his funeral. Ten days before the first CA final paper, Aaji, my grandmother, passed away. I was very close to her, and quite often stopped by her house on my way to class.

She had not been keeping well and when she was hospitalized the doctor had told us she would not survive long. I was aware of this fact but not wanting to break my study discipline, I did not visit her in hospital—not even once. One night, I came home from the library at 11.30 p.m. and was told that Aaji had passed away. I went blank—shattered at hearing this news. I rushed to the funeral ground where the rituals were held—hoping to at least see her one last time. But it was too late.

That night I cried and cried, not able to sleep. I had not taken off a single day from studying to see my Aaji, and now there was no option except to study. I got ready and by 6 a.m. I was back at the library.

The first group CA results were out two months after the exams. The papers had been hard and I was tense, doubtful that I would make it. But just as before, I cleared the exam.

I passed the CA Finals in July 2016! I was very happy with my achievement and so were my parents. Almost every day people visited our home and invited me for lunch and dinner. However, owing to certain professional commitments that needed to be fulfilled, I still had no time to celebrate with family and friends. Once I am done with those, I will enjoy myself!

Yes, a large part of my life has been occupied with exams. It is still difficult to take even a single day off to just have fun. Even Sundays are busy. I do have hobbies—trekking, making Madhubani-style paintings, reading and celebrating happy occasions. And I am still fun-loving, independent, strong-willed, with a long list of friends—from Akanksha, school and college. One day, I will take time out for my favourite activities and friends.

All my earnings were spent on my education, but now

that I am done with the CA course, I will begin to save and support my family. My CA degree has given me scope to work in any company in the financial sector—insurance, banking or an audit firm. I am working with a firm of chartered accountants— auditing, finalizing accounts and doing taxation work. In future, I will always look for an organization where I can freely present my ideas and thoughts, not where I have to blindly obey senior managers. A backup option is to get experience and open a private practice—consulting in taxation, audit and accountancy.

The present is better and beyond what I had ever imagined. At the Centre we were taught to never give up—to try and overcome all barriers. I don't know what my future will be, but I know one thing—I have faith in myself like Aaji had faith in me. Wherever she is now, I know Aaji is happy. She wanted me to be successful—I'm on my way there.

&

'When Papa heard that I ranked first in my division, his eyes lit with happiness. Since then, whenever I clear any exam, he distributes at least five kilos of sweets. After my first academic success, Papa's attitude to education changed and he respected my determination to continue my studies.'

NAVAL SHAIKH | AKANKSHA | 1995 TO 2003

Junior Art Associate

Art for Akanksha

Date of Birth: 25 February 1987

LOOKING BEYOND MARRIAGE

In our community, it is the family elders who arrange marriages. My marriage was different. I did not expect my husband to provide me with a car or bungalow, but I did want a man who would earn enough to keep me comfortable. I fell in love with Eliyas Sheikh, whom I had met through my brother, and imagined we would live happily ever after—like in the storybooks. My mother knew that the boy was not right for me and I was taking a wrong step. But I was stubborn, I was 18, and I was in love.

My parents never came to the wedding reception, but my three sisters were there to support me. Soon after the wedding, I realized that Mom was right and I had judged Eliyas all wrong. His promises were false. He had no proper work, only odd jobs selling ladies' accessories outside Crawford Market—after some time he was too lazy to work and even gave that up.

Eliyas had left school in Class 3 and never wanted to study more. He has a drinking habit and when he drinks, he is a shaitan (devil), difficult to handle. He also gambles, demands money from his mother and me to pay his debts, and dreams of opening a shop with the lakhs of rupees that he imagines I have saved!

I have been married for 11 years, and my mother is always telling me to leave him. But I have a responsibility to try to make our marriage work. And yet, I have a duty to my children, and I know the stressful atmosphere in our home is having a bad effect on them.

Social customs are strict in our community and the wife is always blamed for any marital problem. If I left my husband's home, I would bring shame on my family. My other fear is that in anger Eliyas might harm our children, or carry out his emotional blackmail threats to kill himself.

My children bring the greatest happiness into my life, and I try to be a good role model for them, balancing their father's bad influences. Mehek, my daughter, is 9 and her name means fragrance. She is a serious little girl and does well in her studies. My son, Akib, meaning 'the follower', is 7 years old, and just like his name, he is my shadow and follows me everywhere. He has taken after me—loves art and does well at it.

Eliyas is good to the children and my son, especially, is very fond of him. Both Mehek and Akib are bilingual, they talk to me in English and to my husband in Hindi. I push them to excel in English, because I know the big advantage my knowledge of English has given me both in school and in my working life. Both my children are in an Akanksha school, and when I sit down to do homework with them, my own happy days at Akanksha come tumbling out.

I had a happy childhood with parents who were understanding and wanted us to study. Apa, my dad, had a job in the garbage-disposal department of BMC. To make more money, he also ran a grocery shop, and though not educated, he was good at mathematics and managed the shop so that it made a profit. My brother, Moin, helped Dad to buy the stocks, and the rest of us helped out in different ways. In the evenings, we would sit under the stars, on the khatiya (a cot made of ropes) outside our room, and Dad read from the holy Quran, explaining the Islamic rules on how to be a good person. I loved those evenings.

In 1995, the BMC bulldozers rolled over our one-room shacks on P D'mello Road, and in less than two hours destroyed our houses—making us homeless. We were living in shelters, under sheets of plastic, corrugated tin and bamboo poles, when Shaheen Didi came looking for kids to enrol in the Akanksha Foundation. We are six siblings—five sisters and one brother. Five of us have studied at Akanksha. Sajjida and Naheeda graduated, Najma got married at 13 and Naseema does sewing, a skill she learnt at the Centre. I can never thank my Mom enough for sending us to Akanksha.

I was 8 years old when I went to the Akanksha St Xavier's College Centre—Mondays through Fridays, for two-and-a-half hours every afternoon. It was my first experience in a classroom, and I could not read a simple sentence. Soon after that, the didis got me admission into Class 3 at a BMC School. In six months, I was attending classes in two different places, the Centre and the school, and for some time, I did not know what was going on in either place!

The time spent at the Centre flew by quickly. I did well in my studies, loved the field trips, but I was happiest in the Art class. I was ready to spend my whole life at Akanksha! Encouraged to speak in English all the time, I was surprised at how fast my reading, writing, and *toota phoota* (broken/imperfect) English improved. Since I had started my formal education late, I was behind in the BMC school, but in English I was the star—representing the class when the inspectors visited the school.

At Akanksha we got knowledge from books, teachers and outside mentors. Boys and girls mixed freely, played in the same teams, and were given equal respect and responsibilities. Many of my friends were boys, but after marriage my husband objected to these male friendships, and to keep peace in the house I stopped seeing my male friends.

The BMC schools ended after Class 7, but even with the extra income from the shop, Papa could not afford to send even one of his six children to a private school. Although my mom used her money very carefully, it was not easy to feed and educate a large family in Mumbai. So my education came to a full stop. I was desperate to complete school, but was clueless what to do next until I met a bhaiya called Sriram, who helped me get admission to the NIOS and arranged coaching classes for my sister Naheeda and me. But before I could give my Class 10 exams, I got married, and quit my studies.

For seven months after the wedding I lived with my mother-in-law, and like Cinderella, did all the housework while her three daughters sat doing nothing! We stayed together in a basti (house in the slums) much smaller than the home I had grown up in. My mother-in-law was a difficult woman, though I must say I too was not the traditional daughter-in-law! I have a quick temper, and when my mother-in-law wrongly accused me of something, I answered her right back—and that made her mad. Eliyas made the situation worse, for he was always demanding money; his mother had spoilt him by giving him part of the income she made by renting out handcarts.

My relationship with my mother-in-law got worse, and though my husband often supported me, I was very unhappy. I did not have the guts to go to my mother, but when she heard about my problems from a neighbour, she came and took me to her home. Within a week, Sriram Bhaiya had found a solution—he located a small room where my husband and I could live on our own.

We were happier staying by ourselves, but Eliyas was still not earning well, and Mom suggested that I look for work. Again, it was Sriram Bhaiya who solved the problem, offering me a job as an Assistant Teacher in Akanksha's Supari Tank Centre, where I worked for two years. Eliyas took good care of me when I became pregnant, and at the age of 20 I had my first baby, and soon after that another one. We were now a proper nuclear family.

With two children to look after, my hope of completing school and getting a degree was pushed to the background, and going to college remained a dream.

Sriram Bhaiya knew I was disappointed, and explained to my husband that the whole family would benefit if I could stand on my own two feet, get a degree, and later a good job. Most husbands would have been insulted that another man had dared to advise their wife, but I am grateful to Eliyas for agreeing to let me study for the Class 10 board examination.

Bhaiya knows me better than anyone; just by looking at my face he can make out how I feel. Like an older brother, he advised me not to give up on problems, but to take them on and solve them. Everyone has someone they can turn to in times of need, I have Sriram Bhaiya. A superhero—he appears whenever I have a problem and is also my best friend.

As the children grew up, there were more expenses and I needed to find work while I studied. It was not easy for a 23-year-old girl who had only gone up to Class 7, to get employment. Again, I turned to Akanksha, and got a job as an Art Assistant on the Art for Akanksha team. I coordinated exhibitions, marketed art products, and was a substitute Art Teacher in one of the Akanksha schools.

Now I teach in two Akanksha schools and work in the art store. I follow an art curriculum but encourage my students to explore their own ideas. It gives me the greatest joy to see children freely express themselves through the colours and subjects they like. I too find it easier to talk through painting than through words. As a student, I painted on paper, chairs, trays and tables, now I love to work in big spaces and have been lucky to paint murals commissioned by the True School of Music, the National High School, offices and private homes.

My marriage has ups and downs. Eliyas is basically a good person, but is easily influenced by bad company. Sometimes he gambles, and though he only drinks on weekends, he can become violent and only when I leave to go to my mother's house, he repents and stops drinking. I often ask him, 'What are you doing for us? I work, cook, wash, look after the kids and take them to school.' What can he reply? He does not even look for a permanent job! My children know his bad points well. Ma (I call my mother both mom and ma) wants me to leave him, but I made the wrong decision and I must bear it.

Eliyas knows that if he pushes me too much, I am capable of taking the children and living independently. I do love him and even after 11 years, I keep hoping he will become more responsible. We now live in a proper chawl (a room with common facilities in a proper concrete building) but when his mum gets a house, Eliyas wants to stay with her and his two sisters and their five children! I definitely won't do that.

So when he discusses this, I let his words just go over my head.

There are strict unwritten rules in my community on marriage between different religious groups. I never questioned these, until I took part in an Akanksha musical called *Once Upon a Time in Shantipur*. In the play, a Hindu boy and a Muslim girl fall in love. Both families object to the marriage, but as the story continues, the couple marries and both religions are respected. Seeing the value in different perspectives, I got a better understanding of myself.

Akanksha encouraged us to ask questions and I began to question some social practices of my community—especially gender discrimination. Apa loved us all, but my brother was his favorite. He went to the hospital when his son was born, but not to see any of his five baby daughters. My brother never helped with the housework—only he was given kites to fly and tops to spin. He roamed around freely with his pals while we sisters were not even allowed to bring friends home. But on the Eid festival, we were all given the same amount of money to buy clothes. Unfortunately, my brother did not live up to my father's expectations, and when Apa retired, he took over his job in the BMC garbage-collection department. Both Naheeda, who is a successful teacher, and I, have now earned respect and Apa (whom I also call Dad), tells me, 'You are not my daughter, but my son!'

Although my husband doesn't like it, I make the rules for my children. Mehek and Akib are treated equally. Apart from occasionally cooking an omelette or khichri, Eliyas never helps me with housework. But my son cleans the bartans (utensils) and does the jharoo (sweeping), and my daughter is free to choose any game she wants to play. It is because boys are allowed to be lords of the household that they think they are superior to girls, and grow up to become men who have no respect for women. I know my son will be different.

My husband is old-fashioned and wants me to wear a burqa but I refuse to cover myself up! I choose the battles that I want to win, and give in to others. For example, to keep peace with him, I don't wear jeans at home!

Where will I be five years from now? The answer is—at Akanksha. I see myself as a permanent Art Teacher in one of the schools run by the organization. My didis used to say that when you love what you do, you do it well. I hope my love for art has made me a good teacher. My strengths are in curriculum—teaching, painting, craft activities, mural art, and conducting workshops. My life is richer because of art; I want the same for my students.

Akanksha has become as familiar and comfortable as home; if I make mistakes here, *theek hai* (it's OK). When I need to earn more, I will have to look for another job, but even thinking about leaving Akanksha scares me. I am also not free to choose where I work, for my husband, like the crime patrol, keeps a watch over me and will only permit me to work in Akanksha, where he is sure no one will take advantage of me. So at the moment—I am going nowhere else.

Sometimes, I stop and ask myself, 'Have all my struggles been worth it?' The answer is always—YES. My children are doing well in school and will achieve even more than their potential. I will set no bar for them, they will be free to choose what they want to do, to become who they want to be. I will support them in every step of their lives.

I have, in a small way, had some positive influence in the

community. Many families now encourage girls to get jobs, and accept their daughters' contributions to household expenses. At last, I have gained my mother-in-law's respect! She sees the advantages of an education and encourages her daughters to complete school. Sometimes she even comes to me for advice! I never get tired of telling my girlfriends, 'If you want respect, you have to become something in your life. First get educated, be financially independent, and then think carefully before you get married.' My sister Naheeda, another mom to me, is a very successful teacher, and has had the courage to stay single until she is ready to marry.

Whenever I see children wandering in the slums with nowhere to go, and nothing positive to do, I see myself as I was 28 years ago. It is now my turn to help others. I have started, by contributing towards my dearest friend Sheetal's fees, so she can attend a nursing college.

On 15 April 2016, Akanksha celebrated its 25th anniversary, and my daughter Mehek was the presenter for the evening. She called me up on the stage and proudly introduced me as her mother, an Art Teacher and an Akanksha alumnus. In the hall, were nearly a thousand people—my teachers, volunteers, my friends and students, all clapping... I hugged Mehek, so thankful that I could pass on the Akanksha legacy to her.

∽

'It is because boys are allowed to be lords of the household that they think they are superior to girls, and grow up to become men who have no respect for women.
I know my son will be different.'

ROHIT JETKE | AKANKSHA | 2007 TO 2015
Diploma in Interior Design, Vishwakarma Creative College, Pune
Founder, Vidhyarthi Vikas Vasphith
Date of Birth: 19 April 1998

IN A PAINTED WORLD

It is easy to express myself through art. I paint in the colours that suit my moods—black, grey and dark green on days that I am depressed, red monsters when I am angry, and calm blue seas and green fields when I feel at peace. My interest in art was triggered in Class 2, when I received the Natraj prize for colouring a landscape scene. It was my very first achievement and I was inspired to keep drawing, copying from picture books—trees and mountains, flowers and vases.

When I moved to school, teachers gave me the freedom to draw what and how I wanted. From childhood, I loved to paint and in school they encouraged my passion. I took the elementary and secondary art exams and my techniques improved. It was with Ulas Sir, my mentor, that I did my first major art projects— murals in three schools, a Christmas tree model created from waste products and a 10 ft x 10 ft collage of Sachin Tendulkar! As an artist, I have experimented with different topics, but I am happiest painting landscapes and portraits.

There are not many pretty things to paint in Yashwant Nagar, Pune, but still, it is not a slum. All the families are lower middle class, and we don't have the problems that occur when people from different social and economic groups live together. The men in our community make a living as gardeners and sweepers—some have grocery shops. The women are usually not permitted to go out to work.

The violence in our area never ends. It begins with bullies beating up small kids, and when the kids become teenagers, they beat children who are younger and weaker than them—a circle of violence! I was lucky that because my parents were always around, I was not an easy target for older boys. But that didn't stop me from fighting—I used my fists as often as the others.

People who live in communities stick together, supporting each other against outsiders. Kaka (father's brother) became sick with a kidney problem, and when my parents were in the hospital for four months with him, neighbours took care of my sister, Sneha, and me. We did not have enough money to pay for Kaka's medical bills, and again, it was our community who helped us with the payments.

We live in a proper cement house with two rooms, a terrace and an indoor toilet. My father, who has never been to school, runs an alcohol shop in the open area in front of our home. He makes enough money, but after paying Kaka's medical bills, school fees and household expenses, not much of it remains. Papa's drinking habit is made worse because he owns a liquor shop, and after drinking too much, he creates havoc. Frustrated and desperate for money, he beats up Mummy and the fights between them begin. Everyone has tried to tell him to drink less—he listens and for a short period, stops drinking, and then starts all over again. If he had another job maybe he would not drink so much. Now it has become more than a habit—he is an alcoholic. Kaka says he should go to Alcoholics Anonymous, but I don't think he ever will, for with time, his drinking has only increased.

Mummy, who has studied till Class 7, was determined that

my sister and I must go to college. She worried that Papa's behaviour would have a bad influence on us and wanted us to stay with our grandparents. But their home was far from Sneha's English-medium PMC school, and if we had shifted my sister would not have been able to attend school.

As I became older, the fights at home got worse, and my sister and I took comfort from each other. The tense situation at home also affected my studies. My teachers came home to discuss my poor progress and find a solution that would not disturb my school work. Sometimes, after they counselled my parents, the fighting became less. Much later, when I started my own teaching programme, I remembered the benefits of those home visits and tried to build strong relationships with the parents of my students.

I have no memories of my first two years in the PMC school. For me, there was only one school—Akanksha's KCTVN. After passing a tough entrance exam I was admitted to Class 3. Unlike most schools, where students have to sit in the same seats throughout the year, at KCTVN we sat in groups, and were free to change places whenever we wanted. Today this is not a big deal, but schools used to be very strict and this freedom was unusual—it gave us responsibility to make our own decisions and made us feel trusted.

School started off well, but then things went off track. I thought the way to score points for myself was to abuse anyone who had a different point of view, and to react forcefully to every situation. My 'bad boy' behaviour got me what I wanted, but it also got me into trouble. In fact, whenever there was trouble, I was in the middle of it! With time and reflection, I have changed, and if my ideas don't match someone else's, I hold my fists behind my back, listen with an open mind, and find a compromise. In school, counsellors worked with me on anger management; now, I try to control my temper myself.

During class breaks, I shared home problems, jokes, experiences with other students and built friendships that have lasted these eight years. The KCTVN teachers were ready to answer questions, even the silly and unimportant ones. Each teacher had a special quality—Shalini Didi was calm and positive, solving the most difficult problem without making it an issue; Amar Sir and Kalyani Didi knew how to advise and guide Papa.

After passing Class 10, I had to decide on a career. Art was the first option. I had received many art awards and participated in the Pune Biennale Festival, but event management and interior design also interested me. Confused and unable to decide for myself, I consulted Ulhas Kagde, my art teacher, and he suggested I take interior design. Bhaiya had known me for four years, and I trusted his judgement. I enrolled at the Vishwakarma Creative College in Pune for a two-year diploma in interior design.

It was Amar Sir, my Hindi and Marathi teacher, who made me aware of the many social problems in India. During a ten-day summer camp in Ambi village in Kharvade, I saw the excellent work done at Amar Sir's NGO, Bal Shikshan Manch. Inspired to establish my own NGO to promote education in children living in slum communities, I began working under the umbrella of Bal Shikshan Manch.

In August 2015, I started an abhyas sikha (learning class) for children, on the terraces of my house and a friend's who lives next door. The informal classes run from 6 p.m. to 8 p.m.—the first hour is for study; in the next hour we do confidence-building activities. The first projects were based on the lives of saints and the history of important sites in Pune. Every subject was discussed and then taken forward by the students themselves—making mistakes was part of the learning process. We try to develop academic skills, together with values and independent thinking.

Our kids have already made interesting self-discoveries—students who laugh at another child's wrong answer usually can't answer the same question themselves; team work, with many brains working together, often brings better results than working on your own; strong friendships can help you get over problems; teachers can also be friends. I try to have the same open relationship with the children as Amar Sir has with me. At present, we have twenty-five regular students, from Class 1 to Class 10, but with the support of the community more new students have started to arrive, many so eager that they walk in much before the classes begin!

Seventy-five per cent of our students are girls, consequently, discussions on gender equality, options that girls have today and early marriages are very important. One mother signed up her son for our summer camp, but did not think it worthwhile to enrol her daughters. My didis used to say, 'Take a step when you see something that is not good or right.' My first big step was to establish Vidhyarthi Vikas Vasphith, my own NGO. The next one will be a campaign against gender discrimination.

The going has not been easy. We have had some opposition from children in the community—throwing stones, banging on our doors, abusing our students and trying to stop them from coming to class. One of our girls did get hurt, but the next day she bravely turned up for class, with a bandaged hand. We did consider shutting down the classes, but the students wanted the programme to continue and took on the responsibility for the safety of the class. Meanwhile, a police case has been filed and the classes continue peacefully.

Starting this project has been the biggest learning experience for me. I still have a quick temper, however, it is controlled. If ideas between students don't match or there is a fight in class, I listen to both sides before suggesting a common solution. Amar Sir used to say that it takes courage and patience to stand up for those who need you. I think I have the courage but I need much more patience!

One day, together with my students and volunteers, I will set up similar projects in different parts of the city. Amar Sir, my mentor and inspiration, has become a good friend and is my best adviser.

My mother is my biggest role model; I respect her wisdom and strength. To protect us, and keep peace in the house, she faced my father's abusive behaviour with quiet dignity. Papa never paid for our education, it was Mummy who took loans for school expenses, giving us the chances she had never had.

I still think about a career in Art, but interior design seems a more practical choice. It is a field where I can use my creative skills and earn a regular livelihood.

After completing the diploma course in interior design, I will do a diploma in event management and establish a company to design and manage public and private events. When I have gained some work experience I hope to head for the Arts Institute in California!

To accumulate wealth has never been my main goal. I want to implement my ideas and change the world. The day I graduated from Class 11, I received the 'Be the Change' award for my work at Bal Shikshan. Shalini Didi had tears in her eyes at the award ceremony, probably remembering the boy who always got into trouble, but had finally made it! The award confirmed what I have learnt—when you have a dream, go with it and never stop. I cannot find the words to say what I felt when I received that award, but if I had had a brush in my hand, I would have painted the sunrise as it began a new day.

◦∽◦

'After completing the course in interior design, I will do a diploma in event management and establish a company to design and manage public and private events. When I have gained some work experience, I hope to head for the Arts Institute in California!'

ACKNOWLEDGEMENTS

I am deeply grateful to the twenty-five young writers who have entrusted me with their stories. Their spontaneous sharing and honest insights have made the editing of this book a humbling and exhilarating experience.

Ritu Vajpeyi-Mohan saw potential in the project, encouraged me to take it on, and was on hold whenever I needed her.

Elina Majumdar and the team at Rupa Publications, thank you for your patience with the many changes I made and for supervising the project.

My dear friend, Dr B.N. Goswamy's wise counsel, support, and incisive comments helped to shape the first stories.

The many email conversations I had with Dharen Chaddha were invaluable in putting the narratives in a meaningful context and adding new perspectives.

At Akanksha: Vandana Goyal gave the green signal, Chitra Pandit advised in the selection of the writers and was always there when I called—Help! Anandhi Yagnaraman made the Pune office available whenever I needed it and Reetika Singh and Abha Raja most efficiently organized the photo shoots in Pune and Mumbai. Ruchika Gupta shared her creative artistic ideas and the sensitive insights of Rajshree Doshi, Anjali Sabnani and Manoj Bhaiya helped me discover the heart of Akanksha.

Jigar Patel, a technical wizard, came to my rescue and sorted out the many computer problems I could not manage. He always found time to promptly respond to every query, and stayed involved, even after he moved to the US.

Pervin Mahoney magically appeared to fine-tune the stories—meticulous in her corrections, objective in her comments and so giving of her time.

I am indebted to Khurshed Poonavala, Director, Commercial Art Engravers Pvt. Ltd., for the many hours of creative and detailed pre-press work he put into the photographs.

Rabia Gupta and her team at RGD generously volunteered their services. They worked magic with the cover design and structured the text and photographs giving both the attention they deserved.

What I dreamt of as a cover for the book, I found in the painting by Rekha Parki, an Akanksha alumnus. Thank you Rekha.

This was not meant to be a family enterprise but it has turned out a bit like that! Rishad, my son, was a constant critic, who energized the many drafts with new ideas and was actively involved throughout the project. His sensitive photographs reflect his intuitive understanding of the writers and his ability to instantly communicate with them.

My husband Mehli's patience with the long hours I spent on interviews and at the computer, his thoughtful comments at every stage of the writing, and his total confidence in what I was doing, made it all possible.

The time spent with Samara and Sana was considerably diminished during the editing of this book, but both grandchildren understood its importance and never complained.

And finally, the inspiration for this book came from my daughter Shaheen, who with her love and hard work enabled thousands of Akanksha children to 'write' their own wonderful stories.

ABOUT THE EDITOR

Saker Mistri has been associated with Akanksha since its inception in 1991. A Speech Pathologist and Museum Educator, she has co-authored children's books with Mamta Mangaldas— *The Kidnapping of Amir Hamza* and *The Mighty Tale of Hanuman*—and with Shaheen Mistri—*Miss Muglee Goes to Mumbai* and *Miss Muglee Met Mr Get.*